HENRY V

By WILLIAM SHAKESPEARE

Preface and Annotations by
HENRY N. HUDSON

Introduction by
CHARLES HAROLD HERFORD

Henry V
By William Shakespeare
Preface and Annotations by Henry N. Hudson
Introduction by Charles Harold Herford

Print ISBN 13: 978-1-4209-5460-9
eBook ISBN 13: 978-1-4209-5461-6

Cover Image: a detail of a Portrait of King Henry V (1387-1422) (oil on canvas), Benjamin Burnell (1769-1828) / Private Collection / Photo © Philip Mould Ltd, London / Bridgeman Images.

Please visit *www.digireads.com*

CONTENTS

Introduction

The earliest edition of *Henry V.* was printed in Quarto in 1600, with the following title:—

The | Cronicle | History of Henry the fift, | with his battell fought at *Agin Court* in | France. Togither with *Auntient* | Pistoll. | *As it hath bene sundry times playd by the Right Honorable* | *the Lord Chamberlaine his servants.* | LONDON. | Printed by *Thomas Creede*, for Tho. Milling- | ton, and John Busby. . . . 1600.'

Other editions of this Quarto (printed for Thomas Pavier instead of for Millington) appeared in 1602 and 1608.

All these texts, however, differed widely from that published by Shakespeare's executors in the Folio of 1623, and their relation to it was for long a burning question, as in the analogous cases of *Romeo and Juliet*, *The Merry Wives*, *Henry VI.*, and *Hamlet.* But the problem is here a relatively simple one, and scholars are now almost unanimous in holding the Folio text to represent substantially Shakespeare's MS., and the Quarto to be a surreptitious version of the acting edition, 'hastily made up from notes taken at the theatre during the performance and subsequently patched together.' The variations in the Quarto are all, with the trifling exceptions noticed below, easily explicable from one of these two sources of corruption:

(1) The five Choruses and Epilogue, with three unessential scenes (i. 1., iii. 1., iv. 2.), are omitted. This would be an obvious expedient for curtailing a lengthy play. It is certain from the allusion in Prol. v. to Essex, that these are as old as March to September 1599, the probable date of the entire play. It is pretty safe to assume then that they formed part of the original draft and were omitted in performance.

(2) Several characters are omitted, their speeches being sometimes omitted also, sometimes transferred. Thus in i. 2. Canterbury and Ely coalesce in a single 'Bishop,' though a tell-tale stage direction at the head of the scene describes the entry of '2 bishops.' Similarly in iv. 3. Westmoreland's part is made over to Warwick, while Erpingham, save for a mutilated semblance of his name in a stage direction ('Epingham') disappears altogether. These changes were an obvious stage-manager's shift to reduce the number of actors required. It is less easy to explain why in the same scene a new character, Clarence, should be introduced (for Bedford), and in iii. 7. another new one, 'Gebon,' for Ramburé, and why in the latter scene and in iv. 5. Bourbon should take the place of the Dauphin.[1] These serve no obvious stage interest, nor are they the kind of changes which occur to a botching editor or a speculative

---

[1] Besides the characters mentioned, Britany, Grandpré, Macmorris, Jamy, Messenger (ii. 4. and iv. 2.), and the French queen have no speeches in the Qq.

printer. It is difficult to resist the inference that Shakespeare did perform some slight redistribution among these in the main faintly distinguished parts. But even this was not thorough-going,—witness the inconsistency still remaining in v. 2. 84, where the Duke of Clarence is addressed as present.

(3) The whole text of the Quarto is barely half the length of the Folio;[2] and its brevity is not that of a first sketch, but of imperfect note-taking. It is not an unexpanded germ, but a cento of scraps. Scarcely a single passage of more than a few lines is reported continuously; catching phrases reappear, complexities of thought or phrase vanish, fidelity for a line or two is purchased by the total loss of the following lines.

The date of *Henry V.* falls within narrow limits. The reference to Essex's expected return from Ireland (Prol. to Act V.) shows that it was acted, and in part at least written, between March 27, 1599, when he left London, and September 28, the date of his summary and fatal return. In the Epilogue to 2 *Henry IV.* Shakespeare had promised to 'continue the story, with Sir John in it, and make you merry with fair Katharine of France'; and the promise is so imperfectly kept that it is clear the entire plan of *Henry V.* had still to be formed when the Epilogue was written. But, as we have seen, the Second Part of *Henry IV.* belongs to the latter half of 1598; while this part of the Epilogue, written after the change from Oldcastle to Falstaff had been made, may be yet later. Hence the general conclusion can scarcely be assailed, that *Henry V.* was written in the early part of 1599, and acted with prologues and epilogue that summer. It is probable, however, that a fragment of one of the least striking scenes in the play as we have it was added at a time when the accession of James had given an occasion for complaisance to the Scotch such as we know that Shakespeare did not always disdain to display.[3] The dialogue of the Scotch and Irish captains in iii. 2. 72 f. is not represented in Qq, and the presence of a Scottish captain in Henry's army is undoubtedly surprising after the strong anti-Scottish animus exhibited in i. 2.—an animus not entirely supported by Holinshed. Simpson saw in this colloquy of the four captains—English, Scotch, Welsh, Irish—a dramatic plea for Essex's policy of composing drastic differences, and especially of uniting Scotland with England. Mr. Fleay prefers to regard the passage as an insertion for the Court performance, Christmas 1605, 'to please King

---

    [2] 1623 lines to nearly 3479 (Daniel).
    [3] The conclusion is confirmed, or not contradicted, by other items of evidence:—the allusions in Prol. to Act I. to the Globe (built by Burbage early in 1599); th fact that Meres in the *Palladis Tamia*, 1598, does not mention one of the most famous of Shakespeare's Histories; and the publication in 1600 if the Quarto edition, founded, as has been seen, upon the acting version.

James, who had been annoyed that year by depreciation of Scots on the stage.'[4]

In *Henry V.* as in *Henry IV*, its magnificent and long-drawn prelude, Shakespeare follows the *Chronicles* of Holinshed and Hall with singular fidelity, adding, as there, a few touches from *The Famous Victories*. The 'Harry' of the *Chronicles* is in substance his. Here, in a fuller sense than in any other of the Histories, Shakespeare meant to recall the actual past. It was the real Harry that he strove to paint, the real Agincourt that he bade his audience reconstruct in imagination from his 'cockpit' and 'vile and ragged foils,' 'Minding true things by what their mockeries be.'[5] But these two, the great King and the great victory, exhaust Shakespeare's interest in the reign. All personality in the play is pale beside Henry's, and all event is ancillary to the French campaign.

Even as described in Holinshed the reign was remarkably poor in opportunities for the dramatist, and it would seem that Shakespeare deliberately made light of some that he found, in order to give his heroic subject in its magnificent simplicity full way without the distractions of intrigue and counterplot. The play is strictly no drama, but an epic in dramatic form. Shakespeare seems to hint as much by the use of the Chorus, an expedient to which he no longer resorted when dealing with the vaster distances and the more colossal warfare of *Julius Cæsar* and *Antony and Cleopatra.*

Only one other drama entirely his own—*The Whitens Tale*—contains a chorus; and there it serves to announce an interval of dramatic time far greater than Shakespeare has anywhere else approached. Except in a single instance (Act V.), the Chorus in *Henry V.* announces only trifling intervals either of space or time,—a journey from London to Southampton, from Southampton to Harfleur, and so on. But the Chorus to Act IV. has no such role to perform; and this Chorus, the most splendid and high-wrought of all, serves to show that Shakespeare introduced this machinery not for the sake of bridging intervals of time and space,—which elsewhere his audience crossed 'on imagined wings' with the utmost unconcern,—but as the most obvious means of bringing home the outward semblance of an event of absorbing interest.[6] In *Coriolanus*, in *Antony and Cleopatra*, there are

---

[4] See note to *Meas. for Meas.* i. 1. 68. *Life and Works of Shakespeare*, p. 206.

[5] Chorus to Act IV.

[6] It is curious that Shakespeare nowhere else betrays any irritation—such as certainly breathes in the close of Prol. iv.—at the imperfect resources of the Elizabethan stage. He solved the difficulty here by the Chorus; Jonson, as is well-known, preferred to solve it by not writing plays in which great resources were needed, and recommended his own *Every Man in His Humour* (written before *Henry V.)* in a prologue (1601-1616), with a probable allusion to Shakespeare's work:—

... be pleased to see

brief bursts of battle-poetry exceeding in sublimity anything in *Henry V.*; but that is chiefly because they are penetrated with a dramatic passion for which in *Henry V.* there was simply no room. The subject was epic, and Shakespeare fell back upon the epic poet's method. No scene in the drama paints so vividly as a few lines in the Chorus the transforming spell of the master presence, which made the handful of worn-out men a weapon of adamant against the serried ranks of chivalry:—

> A largess universal like the sun
> His liberal eye doth give to every one,
> Thawing cold fear, that mean and gentle all
> Behold, as may unworthiness define,
> A little touch of Harry in the night.

Henry's own character is devoid of strictly dramatic elements. It derives none of its extraordinary fascination from inner conflict. He is at one with himself. Even the inherited sin of his house, so burdensome to his father, passes completely into the background. In none of the Histories does it play so slight a part. His naive faith in his right to France is perplexed by no scruple about his right to England. Mortimer, the legitimate heir, is never mentioned; and the conspiracy of Cambridge and Scroop and Grey on his behalf is credited to the gold of the French King.[7] Before Agincourt Henry prays that the guilt of his father's usurpation may not that day be visited upon him; but his fervour is not troubled like Claudius' by any suspicion that he ought to resign the usurped throne. Not only is there no foreboding of the tragic Nemesis which the authors of *Henry VI.* read in the impending ruin of the house of Lancaster; we move in a world in which tragic Nemesis has no place, and another, more Shakespearean, conception of human affairs controls the action. Henry is not irrevocably bound by the guilt of his ancestors: his sheer soundness and strength of character emancipate him at once from the inherited taint and the paralysing self-distrust; if ruin follows in the next reign, it is not the guilt of the dead but the weakness of the living that brings it on.

One such to-day as other plays should be,
Where neither chorus wafts you o'er the seas, etc.

[7] Shakespeare's Cambridge hints darkly at an ulterior purpose in ll. 155-157:—

For me, the gold of France did not seduce;
Although I did admit it as a motive
The sooner to effect what I intended.

In reality, Mortimer himself appears to have betrayed the plot to Henry. S. Remy's *Mémoires*, cit. Stone's *Holinshed*, p. 174.

All the other characters serve in their degree to set off the King's; but none are even distantly his rivals. The English commanders, the prelates, the traitor nobles, are slightly sketched, and either implicitly fall in with or but faintly disturb the onward sweep of Henry's course. The conspiracy of Cambridge and Scroop was in reality a dangerous symptom of distrust: a dramatist bent upon plot-interest would have made us tremble for the King's life. Shakespeare announces it with a quiet assurance that there is no danger, for all is known, and the conspirators themselves hasten to deprecate any further anxiety by expressing their heart-felt penitence. The whole episode serves simply to exhibit Henry's bearing as man and King,—the stern Roman fortitude humanised with Germanic pity and regret—when discharging the duty of sentencing an old comrade and friend to death.

The one formidable rival of the King is no single figure, but the 'bad neighbour' at whom he dashes his little force, the assembled power of France. And the French are drawn collectively, in slightly modulated shades of the same conventional hue. The brush which had painted the rival of Henry's youth, now dashes off with far less care and delicacy the foes of his manhood. The vapouring chivalry, the fantastic self-conceit which so fatally alloyed Hotspur's sturdy Saxon strength, reappear with more of blatant flourish in men of finer wit but weaker fibre. The Dauphin, less original than Hotspur, but without a spark of his real heroism, misconstrues Henry as completely; and Shakespeare plays with visible pleasure upon the tennis-ball motive which he found in Holinshed. He makes the English envoys to the French camp deliver a special message of scorn to the Dauphin (ii. 4. 110 f.); and the Dauphin, in spite of history and his father's orders, figures in the French camp at Agincourt.[8] But the Dauphin is only an extreme type of the fatuous intoxication which possesses the whole host, and is chiefly responsible for its overthrow. Agincourt is the duel of Shrewsbury, writ large; with the difference that there is here no counterpart to the pathos of the mourning for Hotspur. A few wild curses and cries of rage suffice to sum up the immeasurably greater tragedy of the French rout. And in the fifth Act the French themselves seem to share in the exultation of England over their own surrender. In painting Henry's own attitude towards the enemy, however, Shakespeare's touch is not quite so firm as when he limned Prince Hal. The speeches before Harfleur to Montjoy, and after the battle, are hardly in keeping with the modesty of true valour which makes him forbid the display of his bruised helmet and bent sword in the London streets. In his actual treatment of Harfleur he shows a humanity not recorded of the historic Henry, who allowed the town to be sacked. On

---

[8] Holinshed relates that 'the Dolphin sore desired to have been at the battell, but he was prohibited by his father' (iii. 552).

the other hand, his ferocious slaughter of the prisoners at Agincourt has
not a whit more excuse in the play than in the chronicle. And it is hard,
lastly, to resist the wonder, as we listen to the bourgeois jocularities of
the last Act, that the consummate master of words and of thoughts, who
had shown himself so easily equal to every situation of statecraft and
war, should become so obviously the bluff, plain soldier in his wooing.
In these scenes we return within a measurable distance of *The Famous
Victories*, where Henry approaches the French princess with—

How saiest thou, Kate, canst thou love the King of England?
Kate. How should I love thee, which is my father's enemy?
Hen. Tut, stand not upon these points,
       'Tis you must make us friends.
       I know, Kate, thou art not a little proud that I love thee?

No such inequality marks his bearing to his own men. The group
of English soldiery in the foreground are, after Henry, by far the most
detailed figures, and altogether Shakespeare's creation. They provide a
new Eastcheap in which the King indulges the humanities, without the
riots, of the old; and one which, in its relation to the old, gives us a
subtle measure of the King's relation to his past. Pistol and Bardolph,
the old victims of Falstaff's wit, reappear in their disreputable decay
with a congenial third, Nym; but Bardolph promptly falls a victim to
Henry's insistence on honour and discipline, and Pistol's moment of
hollow triumph[9] is but a prelude to his final humiliation; while the Boy,
once a promising pupil of Bardolph's, sums up their characteristics at
the outset (iii. 2.) with the honest indignation and the merciless candour
of youth. Falstaff himself was deliberately excluded, and the omission
is the more glaring since the historic Sir John Fastolfe actually
accompanied the expedition, and, as Shakespeare read in Holinshed,
was left by Exeter in charge of Harfleur.[10] But with Falstaff,
Shakespeare must have felt, there was no middle way between
banishment and the old camaraderie. His powerful personality would
have violently disturbed the focus of the play, and threatened the
supremacy of Henry. In his place we have Fluellen, a less wonderful,
but hardly a less finished, creation of comic genius. Falstaff's humour
is a dazzling solvent of truth: Fluellen's a whimsical enforcement of it.
Falstaff's finest jests are rooted in dishonour and breach of trust;
Fluellen's quaint analogies from ancient history are arguments for
valour, discipline, and hero-worship. It was not in irony, we may be

---

[9] The scene between Pistol and the French soldier (iv. 4.) is suggested by *The
Famous Victories.*

[10] Exeter in the play is first made governor of Harfleur and then found (i., iii. 6)
defending the bridge near Agincourt. Can the discrepancy be due to Fastolfe having
originally been introduced and then omitted?

sure, that Shakespeare let him compare Harry of Monmouth with Alexander of Macedon; and there is weighty significance in the grotesque 'parallel' by which he supports it, that' as Alexander killed his friend Cleitus, being in his ales and his cups; so also Harry Monmouth, being in his right wits and his good judgements, turned away the fat knight with the great-belly doublet.'

CHARLES H. HERFORD

1904

Preface

Registered, along with *As You Like It*, at the Stationers' on the 4th of August, 1600, but locked up from the press under an injunction "to be stayed." In regard to *As You Like It* the stay seems to have been continued; but not so in regard to the other, as this was entered again on the 14th of the same month, and was published in the course of that year. The same text was reissued in 1602, and again in 1608. In these editions the author's name was not given; the play, moreover, was but about half as long as we have it; the Choruses, the whole of the first scene, and also many other passages, those too among the best in the play, being wanting altogether. All these were supplied in the folio of 1623; which, accordingly, is our only *authority* for the text.

In the Epilogue to *King Henry the Fourth* the speaker says, "Our humble author will continue the story, with Sir John in it, and make you merry with fair Catharine of France." Whether this promise was directly authorized by Shakespeare we cannot positively say, as that Epilogue was probably not of his writing; but there is little doubt that the play to which it is affixed was written as early as 1597. That the play now in hand was written soon after the date of that promise, and written in pursuance of it, is highly probable. On the other hand, in the Chorus to Act v. we have the following:

> Were now the general of our gracious Empress—
> As in good time he may—from Ireland coming,
> Bringing rebellion broached on his sword,
> How many would the peaceful city quit,
> To welcome him!

This undoubtedly refers to the Earl of Essex, who went on his expedition against the Irish rebels in April, 1599, and returned in September following. That Chorus, therefore, and probably the others also, was written somewhere between those two dates. The most likely conclusion, then, seems to be, that the first draught of the play was made in 1597 or 1598; that the whole was rewritten, enlarged, and the

Choruses added during the absence of Essex, in the Summer of 1599; and that a copy of the first draught was obtained for the press, perhaps fraudulently, after it had been superseded on the stage by the enlarged and finished copy.

In this play, as in *King Henry the Fourth*, the historical matter was taken from Holinshed, both the substance and the order of the events being much the same as they are given by the historian. The King came to the throne in March, 1413, being then twenty-six years old. The Parliament with which the play opens was held in the Spring of 1414, and the King's marriage with Catharine took place in the Spring of 1420; so that the time of the action is measured by that interval.

Shakespeare, for some cause or other, did not fulfil the promise, already quoted, touching Falstaff. Sir John does not once appear in the play. I suspect that, when the author went to planning the drama, he saw the impracticability of making any thing more out of him. Sir John's dramatic character and mission were clearly at an end when his connection with Prince Henry was broken off; the purpose of the character being to explain the Prince's wild and riotous courses. Falstaff repenting and reforming, if such a thing were possible, might indeed be a much better man, but in that capacity he was not for us. So that the Poet did well, no doubt, to keep him in retirement where, though his once matchless powers no longer give us pleasure, yet the report of his sufferings and death gently touches our pity, and recovers him to our human sympathies.

In respect of proper dramatic interest and effect, this play is far inferior to *King Henry the Fourth*, nor does it rank very high in the list of Shakespeare's dramas; but in respect of wisdom and poetry and eloquence, it is among his very best.

HENRY N. NORMAN

1886.

HENRY V

DRAMATIS PERSONAE

King Henry the Fifth
Duke of Gloucester, Brother to the King
Duke of Bedford, Brother to the King
Duke of Exeter, uncle to the King
Duke of York, cousin to the King
Earl of Salisbury
Earl of Westmoreland
Earl of Warwick
Bishop of Canterbury
Bishop of Ely
Earl of Cambridge
Lord Scroop
Sir Thomas Grey
Sir Thomas Erpingham, Officer in King Henry's army
Gower, Fluellen, Macmorris, Jamy, Officers in King Henry's army
Bates, Court, Williams, Pistol, Nym, Bardolph, Soldiers in King
    Henry's army
Charles the Sixth, King Of France
Lewis the Dauphin
Duke of Burgundy
Duke of Orleans
Duke of Bourbon
The Constable of France
Rambures, French Lord
Grandpre, French Lord
Governor of Harfleur,
Montjoy, French Herald
French Ambassadors to the King of England
Isabel, Queen of France
Katharine, daughter to Charles and Isabel
Alice, a lady attending on Katherine
Hostess of a tavern in Eastcheap, formerly Mistress Quickly, and now
    married to Pistol
A Boy, a Herald, Lords, Ladies, Officers, Soldiers, Citizens,
    Messengers, Attendants, and Chorus

Scene: At the beginning of the play, in England; afterwards, in France.

PROLOGUE

[*Enter* CHORUS.]

CHORUS. O for a Muse of fire, that would ascend
    The brightest heaven of invention,
    A kingdom for a stage, princes to act
    And monarchs to behold the swelling scene!
    Then should the warlike Harry, like himself,
    Assume the port of Mars; and at his heels,
    Leash'd in like hounds, should famine, sword and fire
    Crouch for employment.[1] But pardon, and gentles all,
    The flat unraised spirits that have dared
    On this unworthy scaffold to bring forth
    So great an object: can this cockpit[2] hold
    The vasty fields of France? or may we cram
    Within this wooden O the very casques[3]
    That did affright the air at Agincourt?
    O, pardon! since a crooked figure may
    Attest in little place a million;
    And let us, ciphers to this great account,
    On your imaginary[4] forces work.
    Suppose within the girdle of these walls
    Are now confined two mighty monarchies,
    Whose high upreared and abutting fronts
    The perilous narrow ocean parts asunder:
    Piece out our imperfections with your thoughts;
    Into a thousand parts divide on man,
    And make imaginary puissance;
    Think when we talk of horses, that you see them
    Printing their proud hoofs i' the receiving earth;

---

[1] Readers may like to be told that the image is of three eager hounds held back with a leash or strap, till the huntsman sees the time has come for letting them fly at the game. The Poet has repeated allusions to this old warlike trio. So in *Julius Cæsar*, iii. 1: "And Cæsar's spirit, ranging for revenge, shall in these confines with a monarch's voice cry *Havoc*! and let slip the dogs of war."

[2] A *cockpit* was a small area enclosed for cocks to fight in. The *pit* of a theatre was the space immediately in front of the stage. The occupants of it had nothing between their feet and the ground; hence were sometimes called "groundlings." In the text, however, *cockpit* seems to be put for the stage itself.

[3] The *Wooden O* was the Globe Theatre on the Bankside, which was circular within.—"The *very* casques" is, "*so much as* the casques," or "*merely* the casques." So in *The Taming of the Shrew*: "Thou false deluding slave, that feed'st me with the *very* name of meat."

[4] *Imaginary* for *imaginative*; the passive form with the active sense. An usage occurring continually in these plays.

For 'tis your thoughts that now must deck our kings,
Carry them here and there; jumping o'er times,
Turning the accomplishment of many years
Into an hour-glass: for the which supply,
Admit me Chorus to this History;[5]
Who prologue-like your humble patience pray,
Gently to hear, kindly to judge, our play. [*Exit.*]

---

[5] That is, "admit me *as* chorus to this History." A *chorus*, in one sense of the term, is an *interpreter*; one who explains to the audience what might else be dark or unmeaning to them.—*Supply*, I take it, is here used in the sense of *supplement* or *completion.* So that "for the which supply" is equivalent to *for the completing of which.*

ACT I.

SCENE I.

London. An Ante-chamber in the KING's *Palace.*

[*Enter the Archbishop of* CANTERBURY, *and the Bishop of* ELY.]

CANTERBURY. My lord, I'll tell you; that self[1] bill is urged,
　　Which in the eleventh year of the last King's reign
　　Was like, and had indeed against us pass'd,
　　But that the scrambling[2] and unquiet time
　　Did push it out of farther question.
ELY. But how, my lord, shall we resist it now?
CANTERBURY. It must be thought on. If it pass against us,
　　We lose the better half of our possession:
　　For all the temporal lands which men devout
　　By testament have given to the church
　　Would they strip from us; being valued thus:
　　As much as would maintain, to the King's honour,
　　Full fifteen earls and fifteen hundred knights,
　　Six thousand and two hundred good esquires;
　　And, to relief of lazars[3] and weak age,
　　Of indigent faint souls past corporal toil.
　　A hundred almshouses right well supplied;
　　And to the coffers of the King beside,
　　A thousand pounds by the year:[4] thus runs the bill.
ELY. This would drink deep.
CANTERBURY. 'Twould drink the cup and all.
ELY. But what prevention?
CANTERBURY. The King is full of grace and fair regard.
ELY. And a true lover of the holy church.
CANTERBURY. The courses of his youth promised it not.
　　The breath no sooner left his father's body,
　　But that his wildness, mortified in him,
　　Seem'd to die too; yea, at that very moment
　　Consideration, like an angel, came

---

[1] *Self for self-same*: a frequent usage.
[2] The more common form of this word is *scrambling.—Question*, in the next line, is *discussion* or *consideration.*
[3] *Lazars* here means the same as in *Paradise Lost*, xi. 479: "A *lazar*-house it seem'd, wherein were laid *numbers of all diseased.*"
[4] This is taken almost *verbatim* from Holinshed.

And whipp'd the offending Adam out of him,
Leaving his body as a paradise,
To envelop and contain celestial spirits.
Never was such a sudden scholar made;
Never came reformation in a flood,
With such a heady currance, scouring faults
Nor never Hydra-headed wilfulness[5]
So soon did lose his seat and all at once
As in this King.
ELY. We are blessed in the change.
CANTERBURY. Hear him but reason in divinity,
And all-admiring with an inward wish
You would desire the King were made a prelate:
Hear him debate of commonwealth affairs,
You would say it hath been all in all his study:
List his discourse of war, and you shall hear
A fearful battle render'd you in music:
Turn him to any cause of policy,
The Gordian knot of it he will unloose,
Familiar as his garter: that, when he speaks,
The air, a charter'd libertine,[6] is still,
And the mute wonder lurketh in men's ears,
To steal his sweet and honey'd sentences;
So that the art and practic part of life
Must be the mistress to this theoric:[7]
Which is a wonder how his grace should glean it,
Since his addiction was to courses vain,
His companies[8] unletter'd, rude and shallow,
His hours fill'd up with riots, banquets, sports,
And never noted in him any study,
Any retirement, any sequestration
From open haunts and popularity.[9]

---

[5] That is, a wilfulness with *many heads*, and which, like the hydra, as fast as the heads are cut off, puts forth new ones. So that "hydra-headed wilfulness" is but a strong expression for *freakishness* or *waywardness*; the character of one who, drifting before his whims, is ever on some new tack, or is "every thing by turns, and nothing long."

[6] The air is called a "charter'd libertine," probably because it has by Nature a charter of exemption from restraint, or a prescriptive right to blow when and where it will, and cares no more for a king than for a beggar.

[7] He must have drawn his *theory*, digested his order and method of thought, from the *art* and *practice* of life, instead of shaping the latter by the rules and measures of the former: which is strange, since he has never been seen in the way either of learning the things in question by experience, or of digesting the fruits of experience into theory. *Practic* and *theoric*, or *practique* and *theorique*, were the old spelling of *practice* and *theory*.

[8] *Companies* for *companions*. So in *A Midsummer-Night's Dream*, i. 1; "Turn away our eyes, to seek new friends and stranger *companies*."

ELY. The strawberry grows underneath the nettle
    And wholesome berries thrive and ripen best
    Neighbour'd by fruit of baser quality:
    And so the prince obscured his contemplation
    Under the veil of wildness;[10] which, no doubt,
    Grew like the summer grass, fastest by night,
    Unseen, yet crescive in his faculty.[11]
CANTERBURY. It must be so; for miracles are ceased;
    And therefore we must needs admit the means
    How[12] things are perfected.
ELY. But, my good lord,
    How now for mitigation of this bill
    Urged by the commons? Doth his majesty
    Incline to it, or no?
CANTERBURY. He seems indifferent,
    Or rather swaying more upon our part
    Than cherishing the exhibiters[13] against us;
    For I have made an offer to his majesty,
    Upon our spiritual convocation
    And in regard of causes now in hand,
    Which I have open'd to his grace at large,
    As touching France, to give a greater sum
    Than ever at one time the clergy yet
    Did to his predecessors part withal.
ELY. How did this offer seem received, my lord?
CANTERBURY. With good acceptance of his majesty;
    Save that there was not time enough to hear,
    As I perceived his grace would fain have done,
    The severals and unhidden passages[14]
    Of his true titles to some certain dukedoms
    And generally to the crown and seat of France
    Derived from Edward,[15] his great-grandfather.

---

[9] *Popularity* meant *familiarity with the common people*, as well as popular favour or applause.

[10] In Prince Henry's last speech, Act i. 2, *1 King Henry IV.*, he is represented as deliberately proposing this course to himself, for reasons therein stated. So of Julius Caesar, "the greatest name in history," as Merivale calls him, it is said that in his earlier years he concealed his tremendous energy and power of application under such an exterior of thoughtless dissipation, that he was set down as a mere young trifler not worth minding.

[11] *Crescive* is the same as *crescent*, growing, or *increasing*. So in *Hamlet*, I.3: "Nature, *crescent*, does not grow alone in thews and bulk."—*His* for *its*, as usual.

[12] The Poet not unfrequently thus uses how in the sense of *by which*.

[13] *Exhibiters* is *movers*, *proposers*, or *prosecutors*. So, in *The Merry Wives*, ii. 1, Mrs. Page says, "I'll *exhibit* a Bill in the Parliament for the putting-down of fat men."

[14] The *passages* of his *titles* are the *lines* of *succession* by which his claims descend. *Unhidden* is *open*, *clear*.—JOHNSON.

ELY. What was the impediment that broke this off?
CANTERBURY. The French ambassador upon that instant
    Craved audience; and the hour, I think, is come
    To give him hearing: is it four o'clock?
ELY. It is.
CANTERBURY. Then go we in, to know his embassy;
    Which I could with a ready guess declare,
    Before the Frenchman speak a word of it.
ELY. I'll wait upon you, and I long to hear it. [*Exeunt.*]

SCENE II.

The Same. The Presence-chamber in the Same.

[*Enter* KING HENRY V, GLOUCESTER, BEDFORD, EXETER,
    WARWICK, WESTMORELAND,[16] *and Attendants.*]

KING HENRY V. Where is my gracious Lord of Canterbury?
EXETER. Not here in presence.
KING HENRY V. Send for him, good uncle.
WESTMORELAND. Shall we call in the ambassador, my liege?
KING HENRY V. Not yet, my cousin: we would be resolved,[17]
    Before we hear him, of some things of weight
    That task our thoughts, concerning us and France.

[*Enter the Archbishop of* CANTERBURY, *and the Bishop of*
    ELY.]

CANTERBURY. God and his angels guard your sacred throne
    And make you long become it!
KING HENRY V. Sure, we thank you.
    My learned lord, we pray you to proceed
    And justly and religiously unfold
    Why the law Salique that they have in France

---

[15] Isabella, queen of Edward the Second, and mother of Edward the Third, was the daughter of Philip the Fair, of France. She was reputed the most beautiful woman in Europe, and was by many thought the wickedest. The male succession from her father expired in the person of her brother, Charles the Fair. So that, but for the exclusion of females, the French crown would have properly descended to her son.

[16] The Princes Humphrey and John were made Dukes of Gloster and Bedford at the first Parliament of Henry the Fifth, in 1414. At the same time, according to Holinshed, Thomas Beaufort, Marquess of Dorset, was made Duke of Exeter. The Beaufort family sprang from John of Gaunt by Catharine Swynford, to whom he was married after she had borne him several children.—The earldom of Warwick was at that time in the family of Beauchamp, and the Earl of Westmoreland was Ralph Neville.

[17] *Resolve* is very often used by old writers in the sense of *inform, assure,* or *satisfy.*

Or should, or should not, bar us in our claim:
And God forbid, my dear and faithful lord,
That you should fashion, wrest, or bow your reading,
Or nicely[18] charge your understanding soul
With opening titles miscreate, whose right[19]
Suits not in native colours with the truth;
For God doth know how many now in health
Shall drop their blood in approbation[20]
Of what your reverence shall incite us to.
Therefore take heed how you impawn[21] our person,
How you awake our sleeping sword of war:
We charge you, in the name of God, take heed;
For never two such kingdoms did contend
Without much fall of blood; whose guiltless drops
Are every one a woe, a sore complaint
'Gainst him whose wrong gives edge unto the swords
That make such waste in brief mortality.
Under this conjuration, speak, my lord;
For we will hear, note and believe in heart
That what you speak is in your conscience wash'd
As pure as sin with baptism.

CANTERBURY. Then hear me, gracious sovereign, and you peers,
That owe yourselves, your lives and services
To this imperial throne. There is no bar
To make against your highness' claim to France
But this, which they produce from Pharamond,
In terram Salicam mulieres ne succedant:
'No woman shall succeed in Salique land:'
Which Salique land the French unjustly gloze[22]
To be the realm of France, and Pharamond
The founder of this law and female bar.
Yet their own authors faithfully affirm
That the land Salique is in Germany,

---

[18] *Nicely* here has the sense of *curiously* or *ingeniously*, and its force rather qualifies *opening* than *charge*: so that the sense of the whole clause is, "that you should burden your wise judgment with the guilt of making that *seem* fairly and truly derived which is really a false creation, a fiction of craft and ingenuity."

[19] *Whose right* is equivalent to *the right growing from which*, or *depending on which*: the right growing from which, however plausibly made out, would not stand with a plain and honest handling of the matter.

[20] *Approbation* was used of old *for proving* or establishing by proof.

[21] To *impawn* was to *engage or pledge*.

[22] *To gloze* is to *explain* or *expound*, as in our word *gloss*. So in Holinshed: "The verie words of that supposed law are these, *In terram Salicam mulieres ne succedant*, that is to saie, Into the Salike land let not women succeed. Which the French *glossers* expound to be the realme of France, and that this law was made by King Pharamond."

Between the floods of Sala and of Elbe;
Where Charles the Great, having subdued the Saxons,
There left behind and settled certain French;
Who, holding in disdain the German women
For some dishonest[23] manners of their life,
Establish'd then this law; to wit, no female
Should be inheritrix in Salique land:
Which Salique, as I said, 'twixt Elbe and Sala,
Is at this day in Germany call'd Meisen.
Then doth it well appear that Salique law
Was not devised for the realm of France:
Nor did the French possess the Salique land
Until four hundred one and twenty years
After defunction of King Pharamond,
Idly supposed the founder of this law;
Who died within the year of our redemption
Four hundred twenty-six; and Charles the Great
Subdued the Saxons, and did seat the French
Beyond the river Sala, in the year
Eight hundred five. Besides, their writers say,
King Pepin, which deposed Childeric,
Did, as heir general, being descended
Of Blithild, which was daughter to King Clothair,
Make claim and title to the crown of France.
Hugh Capet also, who usurped the crown
Of Charles the duke of Lorraine, sole heir male
Of the true line and stock of Charles the Great,
To fine his title[24] with some shows of truth,
'Through, in pure truth, it was corrupt and naught,
Convey'd himself[25] as heir to the Lady Lingare,
Daughter to Charlemain, who was the son
To Lewis the emperor, and Lewis the son
Of Charles the Great. Also King Lewis the Tenth,[26]
Who was sole heir to the usurper Capet,
Could not keep quiet in his conscience,

---

[23] Shakespeare often uses *honest* and *honesty* for *chaste* and *chastity.* So here *dishonest* means *unchaste.* So in *As You Like It,* v. 3: "I hope it is no *dishonest* desire, to desire to be a woman of the world"; that is, to *get married.*

[24] "To *fine* his title" may mean to *embellish* or *dress up* his title, to make it *specious* or *plausible.*

[25] *Passed himself off* as heir to the lady Lingare. Bishop Cooper has the same expression: "To *convey himself* to be of some noble family."—The matter is thus stated by Holinshed: "Hugh Capet also, to make his title seeme true, and appeare good, though indeed it was starke naught, *conveied himselfe* as heire to the ladie Lingard, daughter to king Charlemaine."

[26] This should be Louis the *Ninth.* The Poet took the mistake from Holinshed.

Wearing the crown of France, till satisfied
That fair Queen Isabel, his grandmother,
Was lineal of the Lady Ermengare,
Daughter to Charles the foresaid duke of Lorraine:
By the which marriage the line of Charles the Great
Was re-united to the crown of France.
So that, as clear as is the summer's sun.
King Pepin's title and Hugh Capet's claim,
King Lewis his satisfaction, all appear
To hold in right and title of the female:
So do the kings of France unto this day;
Howbeit they would hold up this Salique law
To bar your highness claiming from the female,
And rather choose to hide them in a net
Than amply to imbar[27] their crooked titles
Usurp'd from you and your progenitors.

KING HENRY V. May I with right and conscience make this claim?

CANTERBURY. The sin upon my head, dread sovereign!
For in the book of Numbers is it writ,
When the man dies, let the inheritance
Descend unto the daughter.[28] Gracious lord,
Stand for your own; unwind your bloody flag;
Look back into your mighty ancestors:
Go, my dread lord, to your great-grandsire's tomb,
From whom you claim; invoke his warlike spirit,
And your great-uncle's, Edward the Black Prince,
Who on the French ground play'd a tragedy,
Making defeat on the full power of France,
Whiles his most mighty father on a hill
Stood smiling to behold his lion's whelp
Forage in blood of French nobility.
O noble English. that could entertain
With half their forces the full Pride of France
And let another half stand laughing by,
All out of work and cold for action![29]

ELY. Awake remembrance of these valiant dead
And with your puissant arm renew their feats:
You are their heir; you sit upon their throne;
The blood and courage that renowned them
Runs in your veins; and my thrice-puissant liege

---

[27] To *imbar* is to *bar*; that is, to *exclude* or *set aside.*

[28] The passage referred to is in Numbers xxvii, 8. Holinshed gives it thus: "The archbishop further alledged out of the booke of *Numbers* this saieing, 'When a man dieth without a sonne, let the inheritance descend to his daughter.'"

[29] The meaning evidently is, cold for *want* of action.

Is in the very May-morn of his youth,
Ripe for exploits and mighty enterprises.

EXETER. Your brother kings and monarchs of the earth
Do all expect that you should rouse yourself,
As did the former lions of your blood.

WESTMORELAND. They know your grace hath cause and means and might;
So hath your highness; never King of England
Had nobles richer and more loyal subjects,
Whose hearts have left their bodies here in England
And lie pavilion'd in the fields of France.

CANTERBURY. O, let their bodies follow, my dear liege,
With blood and sword and fire to win your right;
In aid whereof we of the spiritualty
Will raise your highness such a mighty sum
As never did the clergy at one time
Bring in to any of your ancestors.

KING HENRY V. We must not only arm to invade the French,
But lay down our proportions to defend
Against the Scot, who will make road upon us
With all advantages.

CANTERBURY. They of those marches,[30] gracious sovereign,
Shall be a wall sufficient to defend
Our inland from the pilfering borderers.

KING HENRY V. We do not mean the coursing snatchers only,
But fear the main intendment of the Scot,[31]
Who hath been still a giddy neighbour to us;
For you shall read that my great-grandfather
Never went with his forces into France
But that the Scot on his unfurnish'd kingdom
Came pouring, like the tide into a breach,
With ample and brim fulness of his force,
Galling the gleaned land with hot assays,
Girding with grievous siege castles and towns;
That England, being empty of defence,
Hath shook and trembled at the ill neighbourhood.

CANTERBURY. She hath been then more fear'd[32] than harm'd, my
liege;
For hear her but exampled by herself:
When all her chivalry hath been in France

---

[30] The marches are the *borders*.

[31] The main *intendment* is the *principal purpose*; that he will *bend his whole* force against us.—*A giddy* neighbour is an *unstable* or *inconstant* neighbour, one not true to his promises.

[32] *Fear'd* here means *frighten'd*. We have it in the same sense in other places, as in *3 Henry VI.*, v. 2: "Warwick was a bug that *fear'd* us all."

And she a mourning widow of her nobles,
She hath herself not only well defended
But taken and impounded as a stray
The King of Scots; whom she did send to France,
To fill King Edward's fame with prisoner kings
And make her chronicle as rich with praise
As is the ooze and bottom of the sea
With sunken wreck and sunless treasuries.
WESTMORELAND. But there's a saying very old and true,
  If that you will France win,
  Then with Scotland first begin:
For once the eagle England being in prey,
To her unguarded nest the weasel Scot
Comes sneaking and so sucks her princely eggs,
Playing the mouse in absence of the cat,
To tear and havoc more than she can eat.
EXETER. It follows then the cat must stay at home:
Yet that is but a crush'd[33] necessity,
Since we have locks to safeguard necessaries,
And pretty traps to catch the petty thieves.
While that the armed hand doth fight abroad,
The advised[34] head defends itself at home;
For government, though high and low and lower,
Put into parts, doth keep in one consent,[35]
Congreeing in a full and natural close,
Like music.
CANTERBURY. Therefore doth heaven divide
The state of man in divers functions,
Setting endeavour in continual motion;
To which is fixed, as an aim or butt,[36]
Obedience: for so work the honey-bees,
Creatures that by a rule in nature teach
The act of order to a peopled kingdom.

---

[33] "A *crush'd* necessity" seems to be a proleptical form of speech, meaning a necessity that *will* or *may be* crushed, or overcome, by the use of other means, such as locks and traps.

[34] *Advised* is *thoughtful, deliberate.* Often so.

[35] *Consent* and *concent* are only different forms of the same word; but *concent* is the form that has grown to be a term of art in music. The idea of this passage occurs in a fragment quoted by St. Augustine from a lost book of Cicero's. But Shakespeare, if he did not discover it with his own unassisted eye, was more likely to derive it from Plato, who was much studied in England in his time.

[36] *Butt* is a term in archery for the mark or object aimed at. The general idea of the passage is, that action or endeavour has, for its rule and measure, obedience, or rather the thing obeyed, that is, law; and this law, standing as a common mark or aim, keeps endeavour from running at cross-purposes with itself.

They have a King and officers of sorts;[37]
Where some, like magistrates, correct at home,
Others, like merchants, venture trade abroad,
Others, like soldiers, armed in their stings,
Make boot upon the summer's velvet buds,
Which pillage they with merry march bring home
To the tent-royal of their emperor;
Who, busied in his majesty, surveys
The singing masons building roofs of gold,
The civil citizens kneading up the honey,
The poor mechanic porters crowding in
Their heavy burdens at his narrow gate,
The sad-eyed justice, with his surly hum,
Delivering o'er to executors[38] pale
The lazy yawning drone. I this infer,
That many things, having full reference
To one consent, may work contrariously:
As many arrows, loosed several ways,
Come to one mark; as many ways meet in one town;
As many fresh streams meet in one salt sea;
As many lines close in the dial's centre;
So may a thousand actions, once afoot.
End in one purpose, and be all well borne[39]
Without defeat. Therefore to France, my liege.
Divide your happy England into four;
Whereof take you one quarter into France,
And you withal shall make all Gallia shake.
If we, with thrice such powers left at home,
Cannot defend our own doors from the dog,
Let us be worried and our nation lose
The name of hardiness and policy.
KING HENRY V. Call in the messengers sent from the Dauphin.

[*Exeunt some Attendants.*]

Now are we well resolved; and, by God's help,
And yours, the noble sinews of our power,
France being ours, we'll bend it to our awe,
Or break it all to pieces: or there we'll sit,

---

[37] "Officers of *sorts*" probably means officers of different *ranks* or *grades*. Or it may mean officers having different parts or duties *allotted* to them. The sense of the Latin *sors*.

[38] *Executors* for *executioners.* So in Burton's *Anatomy of Melancholy*: "Tremble at an *executor*, and yet not fear hell-fire."

[39] *Borne*, here, is *carried on* or worked *through*. Repeatedly so.

Ruling in large and ample empery[40]
O'er France and all her almost kingly dukedoms,
Or lay these bones in an unworthy urn,
Tombless, with no remembrance over them:
Either our history shall with full mouth
Speak freely of our acts, or else our grave,
Like Turkish mute, shall have a tongueless mouth,
Not worshipp'd with a waxen epitaph.[41]—

[*Enter Ambassadors of* FRANCE, *attended.*]

Now are we well prepared to know the pleasure
Of our fair cousin Dauphin; for we hear
Your greeting is from him, not from the King.
FIRST AMBASSADOR. May't please your majesty to give us leave
    Freely to render what we have in charge;
    Or shall we sparingly show you far off
    The Dauphin's meaning and our embassy?
KING HENRY V. We are no tyrant, but a Christian King;
    Unto whose grace our passion is as subject
    As are our wretches fetter'd in our prisons:
    Therefore with frank and with uncurbed plainness
    Tell us the Dauphin's mind.
FIRST AMBASSADOR. Thus, then, in few.
    Your highness, lately sending into France,
    Did claim some certain dukedoms, in the right
    Of your great predecessor, King Edward the Third.
    In answer of which claim, the prince our master
    Says that you savour too much of your youth,
    And bids you be advised,[42] there's nought in France
    That can be with a nimble galliard[43] won;
    You cannot revel into dukedoms there.
    He therefore sends you, meeter for your spirit,
    This tun of treasure; and, in lieu of this,[44]
    Desires you let the dukedoms that you claim

---

[40] *Empery* is, in old usage, a word for *dominion* or *sovereignty.*

[41] Formerly, in England, it was customary, on the death of an eminent person, for his friends to compose short landatory poems or epitaphs, and affix them to the hearse or the grave with pins, paste, or wax. Gifford thinks, and, apparently, with good reason, that the Poet here alludes to this custom. He adds, " Henry's meaning therefore is 'I will either have my full history recorded with glory, or lie in an undistinguished grave; not merely without an inscription sculptured in stone, but unhonoured even by a waxen epitaph,' that is, by the short-lived compliment of a paper fastened on it."

[42] Here *be advised* is *bethink yourself,* much the same as in note 34.

[43] *Galliard* was the name of a sprightly dance.

[44] *In lieu of is in return for,* or *in consideration of.*

Hear no more of you. This the Dauphin speaks.
KING HENRY V. What treasure, uncle?
EXETER. Tennis-balls,[45] my liege.
KING HENRY V. We are glad the Dauphin is so pleasant with us;
His present and your pains we thank you for:
When we have march'd our rackets to these balls,
We will, in France, by God's grace, play a set
Shall strike his father's crown into the hazard.[46]
Tell him he hath made a match with such a wrangler
That all the courts of France will be disturb'd
With chases.[47] And we understand him well,
How he comes o'er us with our wilder days,
Not measuring what use we made of them.
We never valued this poor seat of England;
And therefore, living hence, did give ourself
To barbarous licence; as 'tis ever common
That men are merriest when they are from home.
But tell the Dauphin I will keep my state,
Be like a King and show my sail of greatness
When I do rouse me in my throne of France:
For that I have laid by my majesty
And plodded like a man for working-days,
But I will rise there with so full a glory
That I will dazzle all the eyes of France,
Yea, strike the Dauphin blind to look on us.

---

[45] In the corresponding scene of *The Famous Victories of Henry* the *Fifth*, the Archbishop delivers to the King "a *tunne* of tennis-balles "as a present from the Dauphin. The King thereupon exclaims, "What, a *gilded tunne!*" and, upon his asking, "What might the meaning thereof be?" the Archbishop replies, "My lord, hearing of your wildness before your father's death, sent you this, meaning that you are more fitter for a tennis-court than a field." I quote this mainly as throwing light on the meaning of *tun* here. The following from *The Edinburgh Review*, October, 1872, will give what further light may be needed. "In addition to a large cask containing a certain measure of liquids or solids, it was applied to a goblet, chalice, or drinking-cup, more commonly a silver-gilt goblet. Thus Minsheu, on the English side of his *Spanish Dictionary*, gives 'a *tunne*, or nut to drink in, *cubilète*,' which is explained, 'a drinking-cup of silver, or such a cup as jugglers use, to show divers tricks by.' In illustration of this we may mention that in an old country town we remember an inn formerly known as 'The Three Tuns,' which had as its ancient painted sign three gilt goblets exactly like those used by street jugglers." From a passage given by Halliwell, it would seem that *nut* or nutte was used like *tun* for a drinking-cup or goblet, which in wealthy Houses was commonly of silver or silver-gilt.

[46] The *hazard* is a place in the tennis-court into which the ball is sometimes struck.—*Rackets* are instruments made with a sort of hoop at the further end, and some light elastic material stretched over it, for striking or catching the balls in a game of tennis. So Swift, in his Preface to *A Tale of a Tub*, 1697: "'Tis but a ball bandied to and fro, and every man carries a *racket* about him, to strike it from himself, among the rest of the company."

[47] A *chase* at tennis is the duration of a contest between the players, in which the endeavour on each side is to keep the ball up.

And tell the pleasant prince this mock of his
Hath turn'd his balls to gun-stones;[48] and his soul
Shall stand sore charged for the wasteful vengeance
That shall fly with them: for many a thousand widows
Shall this his mock mock out of their dear husbands;
Mock mothers from their sons, mock castles down;
And some are yet ungotten and unborn
That shall have cause to curse the Dauphin's scorn.
But this lies all within the will of God,
To whom I do appeal; and in whose name
Tell you the Dauphin I am coming on,
To venge me as I may and to put forth
My rightful hand in a well-hallow'd cause.
So get you hence in peace; and tell the Dauphin
His jest will savour but of shallow wit,
When thousands weep more than did laugh at it.—
Convey them with safe conduct.[49]—Fare you well.

[*Exeunt Ambassadors.*]

EXETER. This was a merry message.
KING HENRY V. We hope to make the sender blush at it.
Therefore, my lords, omit no happy[50] hour
That may give furtherance to our expedition;
For we have now no thought in us but France,
Save those to God, that run before our business.
Therefore let our proportions[51] for these wars
Be soon collected and all things thought upon
That may with reasonable swiftness add
More feathers to our wings; for, God before,[52]
We'll chide this Dauphin at his father's door.
Therefore let every man now task his thought,
That this fair action may on foot be brought. [*Flourish. Exeunt.*]

---

[48] At the first bringing of cannon into the field *stones* were used for *balls*.

[49] *Conduct* for *escort* or *attendance*. Often so.

[50] *Happy* for *auspicious ox propitious*, like the Latin *felix*.

[51] To *proportion* a thing is to make it *proportionable* to the purpose. So here the noun means *suitable numbers of troops*; as before in this scene: "But lay down our *proportions* to defend against the Scot."

[52] That is, God *going* before; God prospering or guiding us.

SCENE III.

London. Before the Boar's-Head Tavern, Eastcheap.

[*Enter, severally,* NYM *and* BARDOLPH.]

BARDOLPH. Well met, Corporal Nym.[53]

NYM. Good morrow, Lieutenant Bardolph.

BARDOLPH. What, are Ancient[54] Pistol and you friends yet?

NYM. For my part, I care not: I say little; but when time shall serve, there shall be smiles; but that shall be as it may. I dare not fight; but I will wink and hold out mine iron: it is a simple one; but what though? it will toast cheese, and it will endure cold as another man's sword will: and there's an end.

BARDOLPH. I will bestow a breakfast to make you friends; and we'll be all three sworn brothers[55] to France: let it be so, good Corporal Nym.

NYM. Faith, I will live so long as I may, that's the certain of it; and when I cannot live any longer, I will do as I may: that is my rest, that is the rendezvous of it.

BARDOLPH. It is certain, corporal, that he is married to Nell Quickly: and certainly she did you wrong; for you were troth-plight to her.

NYM. I cannot tell: things must be as they may: men may sleep, and they may have their throats about them at that time; and some say knives have edges. It must be as it may: though patience be a tired mare, yet she will plod. There must be conclusions. Well, I cannot tell.

BARDOLPH. [*To* NYM.] Here comes Ancient Pistol and his wife: good corporal, be patient here.—

[*Enter* PISTOL *and the Hostess.*]

How now, mine host Pistol!

PISTOL. Base tike,[56] call'st thou me host? Now, by this hand, I swear,

---

[53] This corporal derives his name from the Saxon *niman*, which means *to take*; and in the old cant of English thieves to *steal* was to *nim*. In fact, thieves generally, I believe, are apt to take it in ill part, if the word *stealing* is applied to their action. And an experienced English magistrate is said to have remarked, that "of the persons brought before him for theft many confessed they *took* the article in question, but none said they stole it."

[54] *Ancient* is an old corruption *of ensign*.

[55] In the times of adventure it was usual for two or more chiefs to bind themselves to share in each other's fortunes, and divide their acquisitions between them. They were called *fratres jurati*.

[56] *Tike* was much used, as it still is in some places, for a large dog.

I scorn the term; Nor shall my Nell keep lodgers.

HOSTESS. No, by my troth, not long; for we cannot lodge and board a
dozen or fourteen gentlewomen that live honestly by the prick of
their needles, but it will be thought we keep a bawdy house
straight.—[NYM *draws his sword.*] O well a day, Lady, if he be
not drawn! [PISTOL *also draws his sword.*] Now we shall see
wilful adultery and murder committed.

BARDOLPH. Good lieutenant,[57]—good corporal,—offer nothing here.

NYM. Pish!

PISTOL. Pish for thee, Iceland dog! thou prick-ear'd cur of Iceland![58]

HOSTESS. Good Corporal Nym, show thy valour, and put up your
sword.

NYM. Will you shog off? I would have you solus.

[*Sheathing his sword.*]

PISTOL. *Solus*, egregious dog? O viper vile!
The *solus* in thy most marvellous face;
The *solus* in thy teeth, and in thy throat,
And in thy hateful lungs, yea, in thy maw, perdy,[59]
And, which is worse, within thy nasty mouth!
I do retort the *solus* in thy bowels;
For I can take,[60] and Pistol's cock is up,
And flashing fire will follow.

NYM. I am not Barbason;[61] you cannot conjure me. I have an humour
to knock you indifferently well. If you grow foul with me, Pistol, I
will scour you with my rapier, as I may, in fair terms: if you would

---

[57] Bardolph here addresses Pistol as *lieutenant*, though he has twice before called
him *ancient*, which is his proper title. Whether the slip is Bardolph's or the Poet's, may
be something uncertain. So, near the close of the preceding play, Falstaff addresses the
same ensign as "*Lieutenant* Pistol." Also, in this scene, Nym calls Bardolph *lieutenant*;
whereas, in iii. 1, he addresses him as *corporal*.

[58] The cur of Iceland is called *prick-eared*, because he *pricks up* his ears, or has his
ears erect and pointed.—A treatise by Abraham Fleming, printed in 1576, has this:
"*Iceland* dogs, curled and rough all over, which, by reason of the length of their hair,
make show neither of face nor of body. And yet these curs, forsooth, because they are so
strange, are greatly set by, esteemed, taken up, and made of, many times, instead of the
spaniel gentle or comforter."

[59] *Perdy* is an old corruption of *par dieu*, which seems to have been going out of use
in the Poet's time. It occurs often in the old plays, and was probably taken thence by
Pistol, whose talk is chiefly made up from the gleanings of the playhouse, the groggery,
and other like places.

[60] Pistol evidently uses this phrase in the same sense it bears in our time. He
supposes Nym to have conveyed some dark insult by the word *solus*, and he prides
himself on his ability to *take the meaning of* such insinuations.

[61] *Barbason* is the name of a demon mentioned in *The Merry Wives of Windsor*. The
unmeaning tumour of Pistol's speech very naturally reminds Nym of the sounding
nonsense uttered by conjurers.

walk off, I would prick your guts a little, in good terms, as I may: and that's the humour of it.

PISTOL. O braggart vile and damned furious wight!

The grave doth gape, and doting death is near;

Therefore exhale.[62] [NYM *draws his sword.*]

BARDOLPH. Hear me, hear me what I say: he that strikes the first stroke, I'll run him up to the hilts, as I am a soldier. [*Draws his sword.*]

PISTOL. An oath of mickle might; and fury shall abate.—

Give me thy fist, thy fore-foot to me give:

Thy spirits are most tall. [*They sheathe their swords.*]

NYM. I will cut thy throat, one time or other, in fair terms: that is the humour of it.

PISTOL. *Couple a gorge!*

That is the word. I thee defy again.

O hound of Crete, think'st thou my spouse to get?

No; to the spital[63] go,

And from the powdering tub of infamy

Fetch forth the lazar kite of Cressid's kind,

Doll Tearsheet she by name, and her espouse:

I have, and I will hold, the *quondam* Quickly

For the only she; and—*Pauca*,[64] there's enough. Go to.

[*Enter the Boy.*]

BOY. Mine host Pistol, you must come to my master,—and you, hostess:—he is very sick, and would to bed.—Good Bardolph, put thy face between his sheets, and do the office of a warming-pan. Faith, he's very ill.

BARDOLPH. Away, you rogue!

HOSTESS. By my troth, he'll yield the crow a pudding one of these days. The King has killed his heart. Good husband, come home presently. [*Exeunt Hostess and Boy.*]

BARDOLPH. Come, shall I make you two friends? We must to France together: why the devil should we keep knives to cut one another's throats?

PISTOL. Let floods o'erswell, and fiends for food howl on!

NYM. You'll pay me the eight shillings I won of you at betting?

---

[62] Pistol's *exhale* means, *draw thy sword.* So in *King Richard III.*, i. 2: "'Tis thy presence that *exhales* this blood from cold and empty veins." The Poet repeatedly has *exhale* in the same sense.

[63] *Spital* is *hospital*; and *powdering-tub* refers to the old mode of treating such diseases as are apt to infect the Doll Tearsheet sisterhood. Pistol means to insinuate that Mistress Doll has gone to an hospital to be treated in that way.

[64] That is, *pauca verba*, few words.

PISTOL. Base is the slave that pays.

NYM. That now I will have: that's the humour of it.

PISTOL. As manhood shall compound: push home.

[PISTOL *and* NYM *draw their swords.*]

BARDOLPH. By this sword, he that makes the first thrust, I'll kill him;
    by this sword, I will. [*Draws his sword.*]

PISTOL. Sword is an oath, and oaths must have their course.

BARDOLPH. Corporal Nym, an thou wilt be friends, be friends: an
    thou wilt not, why, then, be enemies with me too. Prithee, put up.

NYM. I shall have my eight shillings I won of you at betting?

PISTOL. A noble[65] shalt thou have, and present pay;
    And liquor likewise will I give to thee,
    And friendship shall combine, and brotherhood:
    I'll live by Nym, and Nym shall live by me;—
    Is not this just?—for I shall sutler be
    Unto the camp, and profits will accrue.
    Give me thy hand. [*They sheathe their swords.*]

NYM. I shall have my noble?

PISTOL. In cash most justly paid.

NYM. Well, then, that's the humour of it.

[*Re-enter the Hostess.*]

HOSTESS. As ever you came of women, come in quickly to Sir John.
    Ah, poor heart! he is so shaked of a burning quotidian tertian,[66]
    that it is most lamentable to behold. Sweet men, come to him.

NYM. The King hath run bad humours on the knight; that's the even of
    it.

PISTOL. Nym, thou hast spoke the right;
    His heart is fracted and corroborate.

NYM. The King is a good King: but it must be as it may;
    He passes some humours and careers.[67]

PISTOL. Let us condole the knight; for, lambkins we will live.[68]

    [*Exeunt.*]

---

[65] The noble was worth six shillings and eight pence.

[66] The Hostess here uses words, as she has before used *adultery*, without knowing
their meaning. A *quotidian* is a fever that returns every day; a *tertian*, every three days.

[67] To *pass a career* is said to have been a technical phrase for galloping a horse
violently to and fro, and then stopping him suddenly at the end of the course. Nym refers
to the King's sudden change of treatment towards Falstaff, on coming to the crown.

[68] "We'll live together quietly and peaceably, like little lambs."

ACT II.

[*Enter* CHORUS.]

CHORUS. Now all the youth of England are on fire,
    And silken dalliance in the wardrobe lies:
    Now thrive the armourers, and honour's thought
    Reigns solely in the breast of every man:
    They sell the pasture now to buy the horse,
    Following the mirror of all Christian kings,
    With winged heels, as English Mercuries.
    For now sits Expectation in the air,
    And hides a sword from hilts unto the point
    With crowns imperial, crowns and coronets,
    Promised to Harry and his followers.
    The French, advised by good intelligence
    Of this most dreadful preparation,
    Shake in their fear and with pale policy
    Seek to divert the English purposes.
    O England!—model to thy inward greatness,
    Like little body with a mighty heart,—
    What mightst thou do, that honour would thee do,
    Were all thy children kind and natural!
    But see thy fault! France hath in thee found out
    A nest of hollow bosoms, which he fills
    With treacherous crowns; and three corrupted men,—
    One, Richard Earl of Cambridge;[69] and the second,
    Henry Lord Scroop of Masham, and the third,
    Sir Thomas Grey, knight, of Northumberland,—
    Have, for the gilt of France,—O guilt indeed!—
    Confirm'd conspiracy with fearful France;
    And by their hands this grace of kings must die,
    If hell and treason hold their promises,
    Ere he take ship for France, and in Southampton.
    Linger your patience on; and we'll digest

[69] This was Richard Plantagenet, second son to Edmund of Langley, Duke of York, who, again, was the fourth son of Edward the Third. He was married to Anne Mortimer, sister to Edmund, Earl of March, and great-granddaughter of Lionel, Duke of Clarence, who was the second son of Edward the Third. From this marriage sprung Richard, who in the next reign was restored to the rights and titles forfeited by his father, and was made Duke of York. This Richard afterwards claimed the crown in right of his mother, and as the lineal heir from the aforesaid Lionel; and hence arose the long war between the Houses of York and Lancaster. So that the present Earl of Cambridge was the grandfather of Edward the Fourth and Richard the Third. His older brother, Edward, the Duke of York of this play, was killed at the battle of Agincourt, and left no child.

The abuse of distance; force a play:
The sum is paid; the traitors are agreed;
The King is set from London; and the scene
Is now transported, gentles, to Southampton;
There is the playhouse now, there must you sit:
And thence to France shall we convey you safe,
And bring you back, charming the narrow seas
To give you gentle pass; for, if we may,
We'll not offend one stomach with our play.
But, till the King come forth, and not till then,
Unto Southampton do we shift our scene. [*Exit.*]

SCENE I.

Southampton. A Council-Chamber.

[*Enter* EXETER, BEDFORD, *and* WESTMORELAND.]

BEDFORD. 'Fore God, his grace is bold, to trust these traitors.
EXETER. They shall be apprehended by and by.
WESTMORELAND. How smooth and even they do bear themselves!
    As if allegiance in their bosoms sat,
    Crowned with faith and constant loyalty.
BEDFORD. The King hath note of all that they intend,
    By interception which they dream not of.
EXETER. Nay, but the man that was his bedfellow,
    Whom he hath dull'd and cloy'd with gracious favours,
    That he should, for a foreign purse, so sell
    His sovereign's life to death and treachery.

[*Trumpets sound. Enter* KING HENRY V, SCROOP,
    CAMBRIDGE, GREY, *and Attendants.*]

KING HENRY V. Now sits the wind fair, and we will aboard.
    My Lord of Cambridge,—and my kind Lord of Masham,—
    And you, my gentle knight,—give me your thoughts:
    Think you not that the powers we bear with us
    Will cut their passage through the force of France,
    Doing the execution and the act
    For which we have in head assembled them?
SCROOP. No doubt, my liege, if each man do his best.
KING HENRY V. I doubt not that; since we are well persuaded
    We carry not a heart with us from hence
    That grows not in a fair consent with ours,
    Nor leave not one behind that doth not wish

Success and conquest to attend on us.

CAMBRIDGE. Never was monarch better fear'd and loved
    Than is your majesty: there's not, I think, a subject
    That sits in heart-grief and uneasiness
    Under the sweet shade of your government.

GREY. True: those that were your father's enemies
    Have steep'd their galls in honey and do serve you
    With hearts create of duty[70] and of zeal.

KING HENRY V. We therefore have great cause of thankfulness;
    And shall forget the office of our hand,
    Sooner than quittance[71] of desert and merit
    According to the weight and worthiness.

SCROOP. So service shall with steeled sinews toil,
    And labour shall refresh itself with hope,
    To do your grace incessant services.

KING HENRY V. We judge no less.—Uncle of Exeter,
    Enlarge the man committed yesterday,
    That rail'd against our person: we consider
    it was excess of wine that set him on;
    And on his more advice,[72] we pardon him.

SCROOP. That's mercy, but too much security:
    Let him be punish'd, sovereign, lest example
    Breed, by his sufferance, more of such a kind.

KING HENRY V. O, let us yet be merciful.

CAMBRIDGE. So may your highness, and yet punish too.

GREY. Sir,
    You show great mercy, if you give him life,
    After the taste of much correction.

KING HENRY V. Alas, your too much love and care of me
    Are heavy orisons 'gainst this poor wretch!
    If little faults, proceeding on distemper,[73]
    Shall not be wink'd at, how shall we stretch our eye
    When capital crimes, chew'd, swallow'd and digested,
    Appear before us?—We'll yet enlarge that man,
    Though Cambridge, Scroop and Grey, in their dear care
    And tender preservation of our person,
    Would have him punished. And now to our French causes:
    Who are the late[74] commissioners?

---

[70] *Create* for *created*. The Poet has many such shortened preterites; as *frustrate, situate, suffocate,* &c.—*Duty,* here, is *dutifulness,* the act for the motive or principle of it.

[71] *Quittance* for *requital* or *return.*

[72] "On *more advice*" is on *further consideration.*—*Security,* in the next line, has the sense of the Latin *securus; overconfidence.* A frequent usage.

[73] *Distemper* for *intemperance.* The King has just said, "It was *excess of wine* that set him on." So in *Othello,* i. 1: "Being full of supper and *distempering* draughts."

CAMBRIDGE. I one, my lord:
    Your highness bade me ask for it to-day.
SCROOP. So did you me, my liege.
GREY. And I, my royal sovereign.
KING HENRY V. Then, Richard Earl of Cambridge, there is yours;—
    There yours, Lord Scroop of Masham;—and, sir knight,
    Grey of Northumberland, this same is yours:—
    Read them; and know, I know your worthiness.—
    My Lord of Westmoreland,—and uncle Exeter,—
    We will aboard to night.—Why, how now, gentlemen!
    What see you in those papers that you lose
    So much complexion?—Look ye, how they change!
    Their cheeks are paper.—Why, what read you there
    That hath so cowarded and chased your blood
    Out of appearance?
CAMBRIDGE. I do confess my fault;
    And do submit me to your highness' mercy.
GREY SCROOP. To which we all appeal.
KING HENRY V. The mercy that was quick[75] in us but late,
    By your own counsel is suppress'd and kill'd:
    You must not dare, for shame, to talk of mercy;
    For your own reasons turn into your bosoms,
    As dogs upon their masters, worrying you.—
    See you, my princes, and my noble peers,
    These English monsters! My Lord of Cambridge here,
    You know how apt our love was to accord
    To furnish him[76] with all appurtenants
    Belonging to his honour; and this man
    Hath, for a few light crowns, lightly[77] conspired,
    And sworn unto the practises of France,
    To kill us here in Hampton: to the which
    This knight, no less for bounty bound to us
    Than Cambridge is, hath likewise sworn.—But, O,
    What shall I say to thee, Lord Scroop? thou cruel,
    Ingrateful, savage and inhuman creature!
    Thou that didst bear the key of all my counsels,
    That knew'st the very bottom of my soul,
    That almost mightst have coin'd me into gold,
    Wouldst thou have practised on me for thy use,

---

[74] *Late* in the sense of *recent* or *newly-appointed.*

[75] *Quick,* here, is *living* or *alive.*

[76] *In furnishing* him; the infinitive used gerundively, as very often. *Accord* in the sense of *agree* or *consent.*

[77] *Lightly,* here, is *promptly, readily,* or *without scruple.* So in *The Comedy,* iv. 4: "And will not *lightly* trust the messenger."

May it be possible, that foreign hire
Could out of thee extract one spark of evil
That might annoy my finger? 'tis so strange,
That, though the truth of it stands off as gross
As black and white, my eye will scarcely see it.
Treason and murder ever kept together,
As two yoke-devils sworn to either's purpose,
Working so grossly in a natural cause,[78]
That admiration did not whoop at them:
But thou, 'gainst all proportion,[79] didst bring in
Wonder to wait on treason and on murder:
And whatsoever cunning fiend it was
That wrought upon thee so preposterously
Hath got the voice in hell for excellence:
All other devils that suggest[80] by treasons
Do botch and bungle up damnation
With patches, colours, and with forms being fetch'd
From glistering semblances of piety;
But he that temper'd thee bade thee stand up,
Gave thee no instance[81] why thou shouldst do treason,
Unless to dub thee with the name of traitor.
If that same demon that hath gull'd thee thus
Should with his lion gait walk the whole world,[82]
He might return to vasty Tartar[83] back,
And tell the legions *I can never win*
A soul so easy as that Englishman's.
O, how hast thou with jealousy infected
The sweetness of affiance! Show men dutiful?
Why, so didst thou: seem they grave and learned?
Why, so didst thou: come they of noble family?
Why, so didst thou: seem they religious?

---

[78] Heath probably gives the right explanation of this: "Working so apparently under the influence of some motive which nature excuses at least in some measure; such as self-preservation, revenge, and the like, which have the greatest sway in the constitution of human nature."—In the next line, *admiration* is *wonder*, as usual in Shakespeare. To *whoop* is to exclaim, or *utter a note of surprise.*

[79] *Proportion* in the sense of *natural order* or *fitness.* The sense of the passage is, that Scroop's course is to be wondered at because it is against all the proper *analogies* of crime, and therefore *monstrous.*

[80] To *suggest,* in old usage, is to *tempt,* to *seduce.* The same with *suggestion.*

[81] The Poet uses *instance* in a great variety of senses, which are sometimes not easy to define. Here it means example, purpose, or *inducement.*

[82] Evidently alluding to 1 Peter, v. 8: "The Devil, as a roaring lion, walketh about, seeking whom he may devour."

[83] The *Tartarus* of classical mythology. *Vasty* in the sense of the Latin *vastus; hideous, frightful, devouring.* So, again, in the third scene of this Act: "The poor souls for whom this hungry war opens his *vasty* jaws."

Why, so didst thou: or are they spare in diet,
Free from gross passion or of mirth or anger,
Constant in spirit, not swerving with the blood,
Garnish'd and deck'd in modest complement,[84]
Not working with the eye without the ear,
And, but[85] in purged judgment trusting neither?
Such and so finely bolted[86] didst thou seem:
And thus thy fall hath left a kind of blot,
To mark the full-fraught man and best indued[87]
With some suspicion. I will weep for thee;
For this revolt of thine, methinks, is like
Another fall of Man.[88]—Their faults are open:
Arrest them to the answer of the law;
And God acquit them of their practises!

EXETER. I arrest thee of high treason, by the name of
  Richard Earl of Cambridge.
  I arrest thee of high treason, by the name of
  Henry Lord Scroop of Masham.
  I arrest thee of high treason, by the name of
  Thomas Grey, knight, of Northumberland.

SCROOP. Our purposes God justly hath discover'd;
  And I repent my fault more than my death;
  Which I beseech your highness to forgive,
  Although my body pay the price of it.

CAMBRIDGE. For me, the gold of France did not seduce;
  Although I did admit it as a motive
  The sooner to effect what I intended:[89]

---

[84] *Complement* is *accomplishment* or *completeness*; quite distinct from *compliment.*

[85] *But* is here exceptive; and the sense of the whole passage is, not trusting so absolutely in his own perceptions as to despise or neglect the advice of others; and then not acting upon either till he has brought a judgment purged from the distempers of passion to bear upon the joint result.

[86] *Bolted* is *sifted.* So in *The* Winter's *Tale*, iv. 3: "The fann'd snow that's *bolted* by the northern blasts."

[87] Here the force of *best* retroacts on *full-fraught*, giving it the sense of the superlative. The Poet has many instances of similar language.

[88] Lord Scroop has already been spoken of as having been the King's bedfellow. Holinshed gives the following account of him: "The said lord Scroope was in such favour with the king, that he admitted him sometime to be his bedfellow, in whose fidelitie the king reposed such trust, that when anie privat or publike councell was in hand, this lord had much in the determination of it. For he represented so great gravitie in his countenance, such modestie in behaviour, and so vertuous zeale to all godlinesse in his talke, that whatsoever he said was thought for the most part necessarie to be doone and followed."

[89] According to Holinshed, Cambridge's purpose in joining the conspiracy was, to give the crown to his brother-in-law, the Earl of March, and also to open the succession to his own children, as he knew the Earl of March was not likely to have any. As heirs from Lionel, Duke of Clarence, his children would, in strict order, precede the

But God be thanked for prevention;
Which I in sufferance heartily will rejoice,[90]
Beseeching God and you to pardon me.
GREY. Never did faithful subject more rejoice
    At the discovery of most dangerous treason
    Than I do at this hour joy o'er myself,
    Prevented from a damned enterprise:
    My fault, but not my body, pardon, sovereign.
KING HENRY V. God quit[91] you in his mercy! Hear your sentence.
    You have conspired against our royal person,
    Join'd with an enemy proclaim'd and from his coffers
    Received the golden earnest of our death;
    Wherein you would have sold your King to slaughter,
    His princes and his peers to servitude,
    His subjects to oppression and contempt
    And his whole kingdom into desolation.
    Touching our person seek we no revenge;
    But we our kingdom's safety must so tender,[92]
    Whose ruin you have sought, that to her laws
    We do deliver you. Get you therefore hence,
    Poor miserable wretches, to your death:
    The taste whereof, God of his mercy give
    You patience to endure, and true repentance
    Of all your dear offences!—Bear them hence.—

[*Exeunt* CAMBRIDGE, SCROOP *and* GREY, *guarded.*]

Now, lords, for France; the enterprise whereof
Shall be to you, as us, like glorious.
We doubt not of a fair and lucky war,
Since God so graciously hath brought to light
This dangerous treason lurking in our way
To hinder our beginnings. We doubt not now
But every rub is smoothed on our way.
Then forth, dear countrymen: let us deliver
Our puissance into the hand of God,
Putting it straight in expedition.
Cheerly to sea; the signs of war advance:

Lancastrian branch; as John of Gaunt, the grandfather of the present King, was the third son of Edward the Third. See page 11, note 69.

    [90] Rather odd and harsh in construction; but the meaning is, "at which I will heartily rejoice, even while suffering the pain it involves."

    [91] *Quit* for *acquit*; as a little before, "And God *acquit* them of their practices!"

    [92] To *tender* a thing, as the word is here used is to *esteem* it, to *be careful* or *tender of* it.

No King of England, if not King of France. [*Exeunt.*]

SCENE II.

London. Before the Boar's-head Tavern, Eastcheap.

[*Enter* PISTOL, *Hostess*, NYM, BARDOLPH, *and the Boy.*]

HOSTESS. Prithee, honey-sweet husband, let me bring thee[93] to Staines.
PISTOL. No; for my manly heart doth yearn.[94]—
    Bardolph, be blithe: Nym, rouse thy vaunting veins:
    Boy, bristle thy courage up; for Falstaff he is dead,
    And we must yearn therefore.
BARDOLPH. Would I were with him, wheresome'er he is, either in heaven or in hell!
HOSTESS. Nay, sure, he's not in hell: he's in Arthur's bosom, if ever man went to Arthur's bosom. 'A made a finer end and went away an it had been any christom[95] child: 'a parted even just between twelve and one, even at the turning o' the tide:[96] for after I saw him fumble with the sheets and play with flowers and smile upon his fingers' ends, I knew there was but one way; for his nose was as sharp as a pen, and 'a babbled of green fields. *How now, sir John!* quoth I *what, man! be o' good cheer.* So 'a cried out *God, God, God!* three or four times. Now I, to comfort him, bid him 'a should not think of God; I hoped there was no need to trouble himself with any such thoughts yet. So 'a bade me lay more clothes on his feet: I put my hand into the bed and felt them, and they were as cold as any stone; then I felt to his knees, and they were as cold as any stone, and so upward and upward, and all was as cold as any stone.
NYM. They say he cried out of sack.[97]
HOSTESS. Ay, that 'a did.
BARDOLPH. And of women.
HOSTESS. Nay, that 'a did not.

---

[93] That is, *accompany* thee. Often so.

[94] *To yearn* is to *grieve*, to *be sorry*, to *mourn*.

[95] *Christom* is a form of chrisom. A chrisom-child was one that died within a month after the birth; so called from the *chrisom*, which was a white cloth put upon the child at baptism, and used for its shroud, in case it did not outlive the first month. Bishop Taylor has the word in his *Holy Dying*, Chap. 1. sec. 2: "Every morning creeps out of a dark cloud, leaving behind it an ignorance and silence deep as midnight, and undiscerned as are the phantasms that make a chrisom-child to smile."

[96] The common people of England used to believe that death always took place just as the tide began to ebb.

[97] To *cry out of* or *on* a thing is to *exclaim against* it.

BOY. Yes, that 'a did; and said they were devils incarnate.

HOSTESS. 'A could never abide carnation; 'twas a colour he never liked.

BOY. 'A said once, the devil would have him about women.

HOSTESS. 'A did in some sort, indeed, handle women; but then he was rheumatic,[98] and talked of the whore of Babylon.

BOY. Do you not remember, 'a saw a flea stick upon Bardolph's nose, and 'a said it was a black soul burning in hell-fire?

BARDOLPH. Well, the fuel is gone that maintained that fire: that's all the riches I got in his service.

NYM. Shall we shog?[99] the King will be gone from Southampton.

PISTOL. Come, let's away.—My love, give me thy lips.

Look to my chattels and my movables:
Let senses rule; the word is *Pitch and Pay*:
Trust none;
For oaths are straws, men's faiths are wafer-cakes,
And hold-fast is the only dog,[100] my duck:
Therefore, Caveto be thy counsellor.
Go, clear thy crystals.[101]—Yoke-fellows in arms,
Let us to France; like horse-leeches, my boys,
To suck, to suck, the very blood to suck!

BOY. And that's but unwholesome food they say.

PISTOL. Touch her soft mouth, and march.

BARDOLPH. Farewell, hostess.

[*Kissing her.*]

NYM. I cannot kiss, that is the humour of it; but, adieu.

PISTOL. [*To* HOSTESS.]

Let housewifery appear: keep close, I thee command.

HOSTESS. Farewell; adieu. [*Exeunt.*]

---

[98] *Rheumatic* is a Quicklyism for lunatic.—"*Handle* women" is *speak* of them, that is, meddle with them in his talk.

[99] To *shog* is the same as to *jog*. Generally used with off, *shog off*.

[100] Pistol puts forth a string of proverbs. "*Pitch and pay*, and go your way," is one in Florio's Collection. "Brag is a good dog, and *Holdfast* a better," is one of the others to which he alludes.

[101] He means, *dry thine eyes.*

SCENE III.

France. A Room in the French King's *Palace.*

[*Flourish. Enter the French* King, *the* Dauphin, *the Duke of*
BURGUNDY, *the Constable, and others.*]

KING OF FRANCE. Thus comes the English with full power upon us;
And more than carefully it us concerns
To answer royally in our defences.
Therefore the Dukes of Berri and of Bretagne,
Of Brabant and of Orleans, shall make forth,—
And you, Prince Dauphin,—with all swift dispatch,
To line[102] and new repair our towns of war
With men of courage and with means defendant;
For England his approaches makes as fierce
As waters to the sucking of a gulf.
It fits us then to be as provident
As fear may teach us out of late examples
Left by the fatal and neglected English
Upon our fields.
DAUPHIN. My most redoubted father,
It is most meet we arm us 'gainst the foe;
For peace itself should not so dull a kingdom,
Though war nor no known quarrel were in question,
But that defences, musters, preparations,
Should be maintain'd, assembled and collected,
As were a war in expectation.
Therefore, I say 'tis meet we all go forth
To view the sick and feeble parts of France:
And let us do it with no show of fear;
No, with no more than if we heard that England
Were busied with a Whitsun morris-dance:[103]
For, my good liege, she is so idly King'd,
Her sceptre so fantastically borne
By a vain, giddy, shallow, humorous[104] youth,
That fear attends her not.
CONSTABLE. O peace, Prince Dauphin!

---

[102] To *line* is to *strengthen.* Often so.

[103] *Morris* is an old corruption of *Morisco.* The *morris-dance* is thought to have sprung from the Moors, and to have come through Spain, where it is said to be still delighted in by both natives and strangers, under the name of *Fandango.*

[104] *Humorous* is *freakish, frolicsome,* or governed by whims. Hotspur, having the same thing in view, calls him "the madcap Prince of Wales." See page 11, note 5.

You are too much mistaken in this King:
Question your grace the late ambassadors,
With what great state he heard their embassy,
How well supplied with noble counsellors,
How modest in exception,[105] and withal
How terrible in constant resolution,
And you shall find his vanities forespent
Were but the outside of the Roman Brutus,
Covering discretion with a coat of folly;
As gardeners do with ordure hide those roots
That shall first spring and be most delicate.

DAUPHIN. Well, 'tis not so, my lord High-Constable;
But though we think it so, it is no matter:
In cases of defence 'tis best to weigh
The enemy more mighty than he seems:
So the proportions of defence are fill'd;
Which[106] of a weak or niggardly projection
Doth, like a miser, spoil his coat with scanting
A little cloth.

KING OF FRANCE. Think we King Harry strong;
And, princes, look you strongly arm to meet him.
The kindred of him hath been flesh'd[107] upon us;
And he is bred out of that bloody strain[108]
That haunted us in our familiar paths:
Witness our too much memorable shame
When Cressy battle fatally was struck,
And all our princes captiv'd by the hand
Of that black name, Edward, Black Prince of Wales;
Whiles that his mountain sire, on mountain standing,[109]

---

[105] That is, modest, or *diffident* in raising objections, in finding fault, or expressing disapproval or dissent.

[106] The grammar of this passage is somewhat perplexed. *Being* is under stood after *which*; and not merely *which*, but the whole clause is the subject of *doth spoil*. So that the meaning comes thus: The ordering of which after a weak and niggardly project or plan is like the work of a miser, who spoils his coat with scanting a little cloth.—For the meaning of *proportions*, in the line before, see page 11, note 51.

[107] To *flesh*, as the word is here used, is to *feed* as upon *flesh*; to *satiate*, to *gorge*. So in *2 Henry IV.*, iv. 5: "The wild dog shall *flesh* his tooth in every innocent."

[108] *Strain* for *stock*, *lineage*, or *race*. So in *Julius Cæsar*, v. 1: "If thou wert the noblest of thy *strain*."

[109] The battle of Cressy took place August 25, 1346, the Black Prince being then fifteen years old. The King had knighted him a short time before. During the battle, the King did in fact keep his station on the top of a hill, from whence he calmly surveyed the field of action, where the Prince was in immediate command. When the fight was waxing hot and dangerous, the Earl of Warwick dispatched a messenger to the King to request succours for the Prince. The King inquired if his son were killed or wounded, and, being answered in the negative, "Then," said he, "tell Warwick he shall have no assistance. Let the boy win his spurs. He and those who have him in charge shall earn the whole glory of

Up in the air, crown'd with the golden sun,
Saw his heroical seed, and smiled to see him,
Mangle the work of nature and deface
The patterns that by God and by French fathers
Had twenty years been made. This is a stem
Of that victorious stock; and let us fear
The native mightiness and fate of him.

[*Enter a* MESSENGER.]

MESSENGER. Ambassadors from Harry King of England
    Do crave admittance to your majesty.
KING OF FRANCE.
    We'll give them present audience. Go, and bring them.

[*Exeunt* MESSENGER *and certain Lords.*]

You see this chase is hotly follow'd, friends.
DAUPHIN. Turn head, and stop pursuit; for coward dogs
    Most spend their mouths,[110] when what they seem to threaten
    Runs far before them. Good my sovereign,
    Take up the English short, and let them know
    Of what a monarchy you are the head:
    Self-love, my liege, is not so vile a sin
    As self-neglecting.

[*Re-enter Lords, with* EXETER *and train.*]

KING OF FRANCE. From our brother England?
EXETER. From him; and thus he greets your majesty.
    He wills you, in the name of God Almighty,
    That you divest yourself, and lay apart
    The borrow'd glories that by gift of heaven,
    By law of nature and of nations, 'long
    To him and to his heirs; namely, the crown
    And all wide-stretched honours that pertain
    By custom and the ordinance of times
    Unto the crown of France. That you may know
    'Tis no sinister nor no awkward[111] claim,
    Pick'd from the worm-holes of long-vanish'd days,
    Nor from the dust of old oblivion raked,

---

the day." This reply is said to have so inspired the fighters, that they soon carried all before them.
    [110] *Spending the mouth* was the sportsman's phrase for *barking.*
    [111] *Awkward* is here used in its primitive sense of *perverse* or *distorted.*

He sends you this most memorable line,[112] [*Gives a paper.*]
In every branch truly demonstrative;
Willing to overlook this pedigree:
And when you find him evenly derived
From his most famed of famous ancestors,
Edward the Third, he bids you then resign
Your crown and kingdom, indirectly[113] held
From him the native and true challenger.
KING OF FRANCE. Or else what follows?
EXETER. Bloody constraint; for if you hide the crown
Even in your hearts, there will he rake for it:
Therefore in fierce tempest is he coming,
In thunder and in earthquake, like a Jove,
That, if requiring fail, he will compel;
And bids you, in the bowels of the Lord,
Deliver up the crown, and to take mercy
On the poor souls for whom this hungry war
Opens his vasty jaws; and on your head
Turning the widows' tears, the orphans' cries
The dead men's blood, the pining maidens groans,
For husbands, fathers and betrothed lovers,
That shall be swallow'd in this controversy.
This is his claim, his threatening and my message;
Unless the Dauphin be in presence here,
To whom expressly I bring greeting too.
KING OF FRANCE. For us, we will consider of this further:
To-morrow shall you bear our full intent
Back to our brother England.
DAUPHIN. For the Dauphin,
I stand here for him: what to him from England?
EXETER. Scorn and defiance; slight regard, contempt,
And any thing that may not misbecome
The mighty sender, doth he prize you at.
Thus says my King; An if[114] your father's highness
Do not, in grant of all demands at large,
Sweeten the bitter mock you sent his majesty,
He'll call you to so hot an answer of it,
That caves and womby vaultages of France

---

[112] Another instance of the passive and active forms used indiscriminately,—*memorable* for *memorative*, or that which *reminds.—Line* here is *genealogy*, or tracing of *lineage*.

[113] *Indirectly* in the sense of the Latin *indirectus; unjustly* or *wrongfully.* Repeatedly so.

[114] *An if* has the force of *if* simply, the two being used indifferently, and often both together, with the same sense.

Shall chide your trespass,[115] and return your mock
  In second accent of his ordnance.[116]
DAUPHIN. Say, if my father render fair return,
  It is against my will; for I desire
  Nothing but odds with England: to that end,
  As matching to his youth and vanity,
  I did present him with the Paris balls.
EXETER. He'll make your Paris Louvre shake for it,
  Were it the mistress-court of mighty Europe:
  And, be assured, you'll find a difference,
  As we his subjects have in wonder found,
  Between the promise of his greener days
  And these he masters now: now he weighs time
  Even to the utmost grain: that you shall read
  In your own losses, if he stay in France.
KING OF FRANCE. To-morrow shall you know our mind at full.
EXETER. Dispatch us with all speed, lest that our King
  Come here himself to question our delay;
  For he is footed in this land already.
KING OF FRANCE. You shall be soon dispatch's with fair conditions:
  A night is but small breath and little pause
  To answer matters of this consequence.

[*Flourish. Exeunt.*]

ACT III.

PROLOGUE.

[*Enter Chorus.*]

CHORUS. Thus with imagined wing[117] our swift scene flies
  In motion of no less celerity
  Than that of thought. Suppose that you have seen
  The well-appointed[118] King at Hampton pier
  Embark his royalty; and his brave fleet
  With silken streamers the young Phœbus fanning:
  Play with your fancies, and in them behold
  Upon the hempen tackle ship-boys climbing;

---

[115] *Chide* in the double sense of *resound* and of *rebuke.*

[116] *Ordinance* for *ordnance*; the trisyllabic form being used for metre's sake.

[117] That is, with the wing of imagination. *Imagined* for *imaginative*; still another instance of the confusion of active and passive forms. See page 11, note 4.

[118] Well-*appointed*, as often, for well-*equipped* or well-*furnished.*—*Brave*, in the next line, is *splendid* or *superb*; a frequent usage.

Hear the shrill whistle which doth order give
To sounds confused; behold the threaden sails,
Borne with the invisible and creeping wind,
Draw the huge bottoms through the furrow'd sea,
Breasting the lofty surge: O, do but think
You stand upon the rivage,[119] and behold
A city on the inconstant billows dancing;
For so appears this fleet majestical,
Holding due course to Harfleur. Follow, follow:
Grapple your minds to sternage[120] of this navy,
And leave your England, as dead midnight still,
Guarded with grandsires, babies and old women,
Either past or not arrived to pith and puissance;
For who is he, whose chin is but enrich'd
With one appearing hair, that will not follow
These cull'd and choice-drawn cavaliers to France?
Work, work your thoughts, and therein see a siege;
Behold the ordnance on their carriages,
With fatal mouths gaping on girded Harfleur.
Suppose the ambassador from the French comes back;
Tells Harry that the King doth offer him
Katharine his daughter, and with her, to[121] dowry,
Some petty and unprofitable dukedoms.
The offer likes not:[122] and the nimble gunner
With linstock[123] now the devilish cannon touches,

[*Alarum, and chambers go off.*]

And down goes all before them. Still be kind,
And eke out our performance with your mind. [*Exit.*]

---

[119] *Rivage*, the bank, or shore; *rivage*, Fr.

[120] *Sternage* and *steerage* were formerly synonymous; so also were *sternsman* and *steersman*. And the *stern* being the place of the *rudder*, the words were used indifferently.

[121] *To* is here equivalent to *as* or *for*.

[122] The offer *pleases* not. This use of *to like* is very frequent.

[123] *Linstock* was a *stick* with *linen* at one end, used as a match for firing guns.— *Chambers* were small pieces of ordnance. They were used on the stage, and the Globe Theatre was burnt by a discharge of them in 1613.

SCENE I.

France. Before Harfleur.

[*Alarum.   Enter* KING   HENRY,   EXETER,   BEDFORD,
GLOUCESTER, *and Soldiers, with scaling-ladders.*]

KING HENRY V. Once more unto the breach, dear friends, once more;
　　Or close the wall up with our English dead.
　　In peace there's nothing so becomes a man
　　As modest stillness and humility:
　　But when the blast of war blows in our ears,
　　Then imitate the action of the tiger;
　　Stiffen the sinews, summon up the blood,
　　Disguise fair nature with hard-favour'd rage;
　　Then lend the eye a terrible aspect;
　　Let pry through the portage[124] of the head
　　Like the brass cannon; let the brow o'erwhelm it
　　As fearfully as doth a galled rock
　　O'erhang and jutty his confounded base,
　　Swill'd with the wild and wasteful ocean.[125]
　　Now set the teeth and stretch the nostril wide,
　　Hold hard the breath and bend up every spirit
　　To his full height.—On, on, you noblest English.
　　Whose blood is fet[126] from fathers of war-proof!
　　Fathers that, like so many Alexanders,
　　Have in these parts from morn till even fought
　　And sheathed their swords for lack of argument:
　　Dishonour not your mothers; now attest
　　That those whom you call'd fathers did beget you.
　　Be copy[127] now to men of grosser blood,
　　And teach them how to war. And you, good yeoman,
　　Whose limbs were made in England, show us here
　　The mettle of your pasture; let us swear
　　That you are worth your breeding; which I doubt not;
　　For there is none of you so mean and base,

---

[124] Shakespeare uses *portage* for *loop-holes* or *port-holes.*

[125] To *jutty* is to project; *jutties,* or *jetties,* are projecting moles to break the force of the waves.—*Confounded* is *vexed,* or *troubled.*—*Swill'd* anciently was used for "*wash'd much* or *long,* drowned, surrounded by water."

[126] *Fet* is an old form of *fetched.* Shakespeare has it several times.

[127] *Copy* is here used for the *thing copied,* that is, the *pattern* or *model.*—"Men of *grosser* blood" are men of *lower rank* simply,—the "good yeomen "who are next addressed.

That hath not noble lustre in your eyes.
I see you stand like greyhounds in the slips,
Straining upon the start. The game's afoot:[128]
Follow your spirit, and upon this charge
Cry *God for Harry, England, and Saint George*!

[*Exeunt. Alarum, and chambers go off, within.*]

[*Enter* NYM, BARDOLPH, PISTOL, *and the boy.*]

BARDOLPH. On, on, on, on, on! to the breach, to the breach!
NYM. Pray thee, corporal, stay: the knocks are too hot; and, for mine
own part, I have not a case of lives:[129] the humour of it is too hot,
that is the very plain-song[130] of it.
PISTOL. The plain-song is most just: for humours do abound:
Knocks go and come; God's vassals drop and die;
And sword and shield,
In bloody field,
Doth win immortal fame.
BOY. Would I were in an alehouse in London! I would give all my
fame for a pot of ale and safety.
PISTOL. [*Sings.*] And I:
If wishes would prevail with me,
My purpose should not fail with me,
But thither would I hie.
BOY. [*Sings.*] As duly, but not as truly,
As bird doth sing on bough.

[*Enter* FLUELLEN.]

FLUELLEN. Up to the breach, you dogs! avaunt, you cullions!

[*Driving them forward.*]

PISTOL. Be merciful, great duke,[131] to men of mould.
Abate thy rage, abate thy manly rage,
Abate thy rage, great duke!

---

[128] The Poet seems to have relished the old English sport of hunting, and he abounds
in terms of the chase. In hunting foxes, for instance, the hounds were held back in slips or
strings, till the game was got out of its hole, when it was said to be a-foot. See Prologue,
page 11.

[129] "A *case* of lives" is a *pair* of lives; as "a case of pistols," "a *case* of poniards," "a
case of masks."

[130] *Plain-song* was used of the uniform modulation of the old simple chant.

[131] That is, great *commander*; duke being only a translation of the Latin *dux*.—"Men
of *mould*" is men of earth, poor mortal men.

Good bawcock, bate thy rage; use lenity, sweet chuck![132]
NYM. These be good humours! your honour wins bad humours.

[*Exeunt all but Boy.*]

BOY. As young as I am, I have observed these three swashers.[133] I am
boy to them all three: but all they three, though they would serve
me, could not be man to me; for indeed three such antics[134] do not
amount to a man. For Bardolph, he is white-livered and red-faced;
by the means whereof 'a faces it out, but fights not.[135] For Pistol,
he hath a killing tongue and a quiet sword; by the means whereof
'a breaks words, and keeps whole weapons. For Nym, he hath
heard that men of few words are the best men;[136] and therefore he
scorns to say his prayers, lest 'a should be thought a coward: but
his few bad words are matched with as few good deeds; for 'a
never broke any man's head but his own, and that was against a
post when he was drunk. They will steal any thing, and call it
purchase.[137] Bardolph stole a lute-case, bore it twelve leagues, and
sold it for three half pence. Nym and Bardolph are sworn brothers
in filching, and in Calais they stole a fire-shovel: I knew by that
piece of service the men would carry coals.[138] They would have me
as familiar with men's pockets as their gloves or their
handkerchiefs: which makes much against my manhood, if I
should take from another's pocket to put into mine; for it is plain
pocketing up of wrongs.[139] I must leave them, and seek some better
service: their villainy goes against my weak stomach, and therefore
I must cast it up. [*Exit.*]

[*Re-enter* FLUELLEN, GOWER *following.*]

---

[132] *Bawcock* and *chuck* were terms of playful familiarity or endearment; the one
being from the French *beau coq*, the other a corruption of *chicken*.

[133] A *swasher* is a *swaggerer*, *blusterer*, or *braggart*.

[134] An *antic* is a *buffoon*. The word was also used of certain pictured oddities, such
as would now be called *caricatures*.

[135] Has plenty of valour in his face, but none in his heart, and so fights with looks,
not with blows; that is, substitutes impudence for valour. *White-liver d* was a common
epithet for a coward.

[136] "The *best* men" are the *bravest* men, in Nym's dialect. So, a little after, "*good*
deeds" are *brave* deeds.

[137] Purchase was a word of equivocal meaning in Shakespeare's time, and was often
used as a euphemism for *theft*.

[138] As *carrying coals* was the lowest office in ancient households, the phrase
became a proverb of reproach. So, in *Romeo and Juliet*, i. 1, Sampson says to his fellow-
servant, "Gregory, o' my word, we'll not *carry coals*"; meaning that, if that reproach be
spit at him, he will fight.

[139] "Pocketing-up of wrongs" is an old phrase for putting up with insults instead of
resenting them.

GOWER. Captain Fluellen, you must come presently to the mines; the Duke of Gloucester would speak with you.

FLUELLEN. To the mines! tell you the duke, it is not so good to come to the mines; for, look you, the mines is not according to the disciplines of the war: the concavities of it is not sufficient; for, look you, the athversary, you may discuss unto the duke, look you, is diggt himself[140] four yard under the countermines: by Cheshu, I think 'a will plough up all, if there is not better directions.

GOWER. The Duke of Gloucester, to whom the order of the siege is given, is altogether directed by an Irishman, a very valiant gentleman, i'faith.

FLUELLEN. It is Captain Macmorris, is it not?

GOWER. I think it be.

FLUELLEN. By Cheshu, he is an ass, as in the world: I will verify as much in his beard: be has no more directions in the true disciplines of the wars, look you, of the Roman disciplines, than is a puppy-dog.

[*Enter* MACMORRIS *and* CAPTAIN JAMY.]

GOWER. Here 'a comes; and the Scots captain, Captain Jamy, with him.

FLUELLEN. Captain Jamy is a marvellous falourous gentleman, that is certain; and of great expedition and knowledge in th' aunchient wars, upon my particular knowledge of his directions: by Cheshu, he will maintain his argument as well as any military man in the world, in the disciplines of the pristine wars of the Romans.

JAMY. I say gud-day, Captain Fluellen.

FLUELLEN. God-den[141] to your worship, good Captain James.

GOWER. How now, Captain Macmorris! have you quit the mines? have the pioneers[142] given o'er?

MACMORRIS. By Chrish, la! tish ill done: the work ish give over, the trompet sound the retreat. By my hand, I swear, and my father's soul, the work ish ill done; it ish give over: I would have blowed up the town, so Chrish save me, la! in an hour: O, tish ill done, tish ill done; by my hand, tish ill done!

FLUELLEN. Captain Macmorris, I beseech you now, will you vouchsafe me, look you, a few disputations with you, as partly touching or concerning the disciplines of the war, the Roman wars,

---

[140] Has *dug his mines.* Properly the order of the words should be reversed; as it is the besiegers who *mine,* and the besieged who *countermine.*

[141] *Good-den* or *god-den* was a familiar corruption of *good day.*

[142] Pioneers are a class of soldiers who take the lead in siege operations; military engineers.

in the way of argument, look you, and friendly communication; partly to satisfy my opinion, and partly for the satisfaction, look you, of my mind, as touching the direction of the military discipline; that is the point.

JAMY. It sall be vary gud, gud feith, gud captains bath: and I sall quit you with gud leve,[143] as I may pick occasion; that sall I, marry.

MACMORRIS. It is no time to discourse, so Chrish save me: the day is hot, and the weather, and the wars, and the King, and the dukes: it is no time to discourse. The town is beseeched,[144] and the trumpet call us to the breach; and we talk, and, be Chrish, do nothing: 'tis shame for us all: so God sa' me, 'tis shame to stand still; it is shame, by my hand: and there is throats to be cut, and works to be done; and there ish nothing done, so Chrish sa' me, la!

JAMY. By the mess, ere theise eyes of mine take themselves to slomber, ay'll de gud service, or ay'll lig[145] i' the grund for it; ay, or go to death; and ay'll pay't as valourously as I may, that sall I suerly do, that is the breff and the long. Marry, I wad full fain hear some question[146] 'tween you tway.

FLUELLEN. Captain Macmorris, I think, look you, under your correction, there is not many of your nation—

MACMORRIS. Of my nation! What ish my nation? Ish a villain, and a bastard, and a knave, and a rascal. What ish my nation? Who talks of my nation?

FLUELLEN. Look you, if you take the matter otherwise than is meant, Captain Macmorris, peradventure I shall think you do not use me with that affability as in discretion you ought to use me, look you: being as good a man as yourself, both in the disciplines of war, and in the derivation of my birth, and in other particularities.

MACMORRIS. I do not know you so good a man as myself: so Chrish save me, I will cut off your head.

GOWER. Gentlemen both, you will mistake each other.

JAMY. A! that's a foul fault. [*A parley sounded.*]

GOWER. The town sounds a parley.

FLUELLEN. Captain Macmorris, when there is more better opportunity to be required, look you, I will be so bold as to tell you I know the disciplines of war; and there is an end. [*Exeunt.*]

---

[143] I shall, with your permission, *requite you*; that is, *answer you*.

[144] Captain Macmorris means, apparently, not that the town is *besieged*, for that has been going on for some time, but that it is summoned or challenged to surrender.

[145] *Lig* is the valiant and argumentative Scotchman's word for *lie*.

[146] Here, as often, *question* is *talk*, *discourse*, or *conversation*.

SCENE II.

The Same. Before the gates of Harfleur.

[*The Governor and some Citizens on the walls; the English Forces below. Enter* KING HENRY *and his Train.*]

KING HENRY V. How yet resolves the governor of the town?
    This is the latest parle we will admit;
    Therefore to our best mercy give yourselves;
    Or like to men proud of destruction
    Defy us to our worst: for, as I am a soldier,
    A name that in my thoughts becomes me best,
    If I begin the battery once again,
    I will not leave the half-achieved Harfleur
    Till in her ashes she lie buried.
    The gates of mercy shall be all shut up,
    And the flesh'd soldier,[147]—rough and hard of heart,—
    In liberty of bloody hand shall range
    With conscience wide as hell, mowing like grass
    Your fresh-fair virgins and your flowering infants.
    What is it then to me, if impious war,—
    Array'd in flames like to the prince of fiends,—
    Do, with his smirch'd complexion, all fell feats
    Enlink'd to waste and desolation?
    What is't to me, when you yourselves are cause,
    If your pure maidens fall into the hand
    Of hot and forcing violation?
    What rein can hold licentious wickedness
    When down the hill he holds his fierce career?
    We may as bootless spend our vain command
    Upon the enraged soldiers in their spoil
    As send precepts to the leviathan
    To come ashore. Therefore, you men of Harfleur,
    Take pity of your town and of[148] your people,
    Whiles yet my soldiers are in my command;
    Whiles yet the cool and temperate wind of grace
    O'erblows[149] the filthy and contagious clouds

---

[147] *Flesh'd*, here, is *made* fierce, as bloodhounds are by the taste or smell of blood. Probably the sense of being seasoned or indurated with acts of cruelty is also involved. So in *Richard III.*, iv. 3: "Dighton and Forrest, whom I did suborn to do this ruthless piece of butchery, albeit they were *flesh'd* villains, bloody dogs," &c.

[148] *Of and on* were used indifferently in such cases.

[149] To *overblow*, here, is to *blow* or *drive away*, or *keep off*.

Of heady murder, spoil and villainy.
If not, why, in a moment look to see
The blind and bloody soldier with foul hand
Defile the locks of your shrill-shrieking daughters;
Your fathers taken by the silver beards,
And their most reverend heads dash'd to the walls,
Your naked infants spitted[150] upon pikes,
Whiles the mad mothers with their howls confused
Do break the clouds, as did the wives of Jewry
At Herod's bloody-hunting slaughtermen.
What say you? will you yield, and this avoid,
Or, guilty in defence, be thus destroy'd?

GOVERNOR. Our expectation hath this day an end:
The Dauphin, whom of succors we entreated,
Returns us that his powers are yet not ready
To raise so great a siege. Therefore, great King,
We yield our town and lives to thy soft mercy.
Enter our gates; dispose of us and ours;
For we no longer are defensible.[151]

KING HENRY V. Open your gates.—Come, uncle Exeter,
Go you and enter Harfleur; there remain,
And fortify it strongly 'gainst the French:
Use mercy to them all. For us, dear uncle,—
The winter coming on and sickness growing
Upon our soldiers,—we'll retire to Calais.
To-night in Harfleur we will be your guest;
To-morrow for the march are we addrest.

[*Flourish. The King and his Train enter the town.*]

---

[150] A *spit* was an iron rod, to thrust through a fowl or piece of meat, so as to place it before the fire, and keep it turning till roasted. Hence the phrase "done to a turn." The word came to be used, as here, in a more general application.

[151] *Defensible* for *defensive*, or *capable of defence*; the passive form with the active sense. So in many words.

SCENE III.

Rouen. A Room in the Palace.

[*Enter* KATHARINE *and* ALICE.[152]]

KATHARINE. *Alice, tu as été en Angleterre, et tu parles bien le langage.*
ALICE. *Un peu, madame.*
KATHARINE. *Je te prie, m'enseignez: il faut que j'apprenne à parler. Comment appelez-vous la main en Anglais?*
ALICE. *La main? elle est appelée* de hand.
KATHARINE. De hand. *Et les doigts?*
ALICE. *Les doigts? ma foi, j'oublie les doigts; mais je me souviendrai. Les doigts? je pense qu'ils sont appelés* de fingres; *oui,* de fingres.
KATHARINE. *La main,* de hand; *les doigts,* de fingres. *Je pense que je suis le bon écolier; j'ai gagné deux mots d'Anglais vitement. Comment appelez-vous les ongles?*
ALICE. *Les ongles? nous les appelons* de nails.
KATHARINE. De nails. *Ecoutez; dites-moi, si je parle bien:* de hand, de fingres, *et* de nails.
ALICE. *C'est bien dit, madame; il est fort bon Anglais.*
KATHARINE. *Dites-moi l'Anglais pour le bras.*
ALICE. De arm, *madame.*
KATHARINE. *Et le coude?*
ALICE. De elbow.
KATHARINE. De elbow. *Je m'en fais la répétition de tous les mots que vous m'avez appris dès à présent.*
ALICE. *Il est trop difficile, madame, comme je pense.*
KATHARINE. *Excusez-moi, Alice; écoutez:* de hand, de fingres, de nails, de arma, de bilbow.
ALICE. De elbow, *madame.*
KATHARINE. *O Seigneur Dieu, je m'en oublie!* de elbow. *Comment appelez-vous le col?*
ALICE. De neck, *madame.*
KATHARINE. De nick. *Et le menton?*
ALICE. De chin.

---

[152] The dramatic purpose of this scene, if it have any, is not very obvious. But there is something of humour, at least there would be to an English audience, in the compliments Alice bestows upon the Princess in assuring her that she speaks English as well as the English themselves. And there is still more of humour *implied* in the act of thus preparing a conquest of France by introducing a French Princess learning to chop English. As the marriage is an essential part of the dramatic argument, it was doubtless in keeping with the Poet's method to represent Catharine in the process of learning the hero's tongue; which could only be done by mixing up the two languages in a scene or two.

KATHARINE. De sin. *Le col*, de nick; *le menton*, de sin.

ALICE. *Oui. Sauf votre honneur, en vérité, vous prononcez les mots aussi droit que les natifs d'Angleterre.*

KATHARINE. *Je ne doute point d'apprendre, par la grace de Dieu, et en peu de temps.*

ALICE. *N'avez vous pas déjà oublié ce que je vous ai enseigné?*

KATHARINE. *Non, je réciterai à vous promptement*: de hand, de fingres, de mails—

ALICE. De nails, *madame*.

KATHARINE. De nails, de arm, de ilbow.

ALICE. *Sauf votre honneur*, de elbow.

KATHARINE. *Ainsi dis-je*; de elbow, de nick, *et* de sin. *Comment appelez-vous le pied et la robe?*

ALICE. De foot, *madame*; *et* de coun.

KATHARINE. De foot *et* de coun! *O Seigneur Dieu! ce sont mots de son mauvais, corruptible, gros, et impudique, et non pour les dames d'honneur d'user: je ne voudrais prononcer ces mots devant les seigneurs de France pour tout le monde. Il faut de foot et de coun néanmoins. Je réciterai une autre fois ma leçon ensemble*: de hand, de fingres, de nails, de arm, de elbow, de nick, de sin, de foot, de coun.

ALICE. *Excellent, madame!*

KATHARINE. *C'est assez pour une fois: allons-nous à dìner.* [*Exeunt.*]

SCENE IV.

The Same. Another Room in the Same.

[*Enter the* KING OF FRANCE, *the* DAUPHIN, *the* DUKE OF BOURBON, *the Constable of France, and others.*]

KING OF FRANCE. 'Tis certain he hath pass'd the river Somme.

CONSTABLE. And if he be not fought withal, my lord,
        Let us not live in France; let us quit all
        And give our vineyards to a barbarous people.

DAUPHIN. *O Dieu vivant!* shall a few sprays[153] of us,
        The emptying of our fathers' luxury,
        Our scions, put in wild and savage stock,
        Spirt up so suddenly into the clouds,
        And overlook their grafters?

BOURBON. Normans, but bastard Normans, Norman bastards!
        Mort de ma vie! if they march along

---

[153] *Sprays* is *shoots*, *sprigs*, or *sprouts*; alluding to the origin of the Anglo-Norman stock.

Unfought withal, but I will sell my dukedom,
To buy a slobbery and a dirty farm
In that nook-shotten[154] isle of Albion.
CONSTABLE. *Dieu de batailles*! where have they this mettle?
Is not their climate foggy, raw and dull,
On whom, as in despite, the sun looks pale,
Killing their fruit with frowns? Can sodden water,
A drench for sur-rein'd jades,[155] their barley-broth,
Decoct their cold blood to such valiant heat?
And shall our quick blood, spirited with wine,
Seem frosty? O, for honour of our land,
Let us not hang like roping icicles
Upon our houses' thatch, whiles a more frosty people
Sweat drops of gallant youth in our rich fields,—
Poor we may call them in their native lords!
DAUPHIN. By faith and honour,
Our madams mock at us, and plainly say
Our mettle is bred out and they will give
Their bodies to the lust of English youth
To new-store France with bastard warriors.
BOURBON. They bid us to the English dancing-schools,
And teach lavoltas high and swift corantos;[156]
Saying our grace is only in our heels,
And that we are most lofty runaways.
KING OF FRANCE. Where is Montjoy the herald? speed him hence:
Let him greet England with our sharp defiance.—
Up, princes! and, with spirit of honour edged
More sharper than your swords, hie to the field:
Charles Delabreth,[157] High-Constable of France;
You Dukes of Orleans, Bourbon, and of Berri,
Alençon, Brabant, Bar, and Burgundy;

---

[154] *Shotten* signifies any thing projected; so *nook-shotten isle* is an isle that shoots out into capes, promontories, and necks of land, the very figure of Great Britain.

[155] *Sur-rein'd* is probably *over-ridden* or over-strained. It was common to give horses, over-ridden or feverish, ground malt and hot water mixed, which was called a mash.—Barley-broth is probably meant as a Frenchman's sneer at English *ale*, or *beer*.

[156] The *coranto* was a lively dance for two persons.—The *lavolta* was a dance of Italian origin, and seems to have been something like the modern waltz, only, perhaps, rather more so. It is thus described by Sir John Davies:

A lofty jumping, or a leaping round,
Where arm in arm two dancers are entwin'd,
And whirl themselves with strict embracements bound,
And still their feet an anapest do sound.

[157] This should be Charles D'Albret; but the metre would not admit of the change. Shakespeare followed Holinshed, who calls him *Delabreth*.

Jaques Chatillon, Rambures, Vaudemont,
Beaumont, Grandpré, Roussi, and Fauconberg,
Foix, Lestrale, Bouciqualt, and Charolois;
High dukes, great princes, barons, lords and knights,
For your great seats now quit[158] you of great shames.
Bar Harry England, that sweeps through our land
With pennons painted in the blood of Harfleur:
Rush on his host, as doth the melted snow
Upon the valleys, whose low vassal seat
The Alps doth spit and void his rheum upon:
Go down upon him,—you have power enough,—
And in a captive chariot into Rouen
Bring him our prisoner.
CONSTABLE. This becomes the great.
Sorry am I his numbers are so few,
His soldiers sick and famish'd in their march,
For I am sure, when he shall see our army,
He'll drop his heart into the sink of fear
And for achievement offer us his ransom.[159]
KING OF FRANCE. Therefore, lord constable, haste on Montjoy.
And let him say to England that we send
To know what willing ransom he will give.—
Prince Dauphin, you shall stay with us in Rouen.
DAUPHIN. Not so, I do beseech your majesty.
KING OF FRANCE. Be patient, for you shall remain with us.—
Now forth, lord constable and princes all,
And quickly bring us word of England's fall. [*Exeunt.*]

SCENE V.

The English camp in Picardy.

[*Enter, severally,* GOWER *and* FLUELLEN.]

GOWER. How now, Captain Fluellen! come you from the bridge?
FLUELLEN. I assure you, there is very excellent services committed at
the pridge.[160]

---

[158] *Quit* for *acquit*; the sense being clear, release, or exonerate *yourselves*.

[159] That is, *instead of achieving* a victory over us, make a proposal to buy himself off with a ransom.

[160] After Henry had passed the Somme, the French endeavoured to intercept him in his passage to Calais; and for that purpose attempted to break down the only bridge that there was over the small river of Ternois. But Henry, having notice of their design, sent a part of his troops before him, who, attacking and putting the French to flight, preserved the bridge till the whole English army arrived and passed over it.

GOWER. Is the Duke of Exeter safe?

FLUELLEN. The Duke of Exeter is as magnanimous as Agamemnon; and a man that I love and honour with my soul, and my heart, and my duty, and my life, and my living, and my uttermost power: he is not—God be praised and blessed!—any hurt in the world; but keeps the pridge most valiantly, with excellent discipline. There is an aunchient lieutenant there at the pridge,—I think in my very conscience he is as valiant a man as Mark Antony; and he is a man of no estimation in the 'orld; but did see him do as gallant service.

GOWER. What do you call him?

FLUELLEN. He is called Aunchient Pistol.

GOWER. I know him not.

[*Enter* PISTOL.]

FLUELLEN. Here is the man.

PISTOL. Captain, I thee beseech to do me favours:
The Duke of Exeter doth love thee well.

FLUELLEN. Ay, I praise God; and I have merited some love at his hands.

PISTOL. Bardolph, a soldier, firm and sound of heart,
Of buxom[161] valour, hath, by cruel fate,
And giddy Fortune's furious fickle wheel,—
That goddess blind,
That stands upon the rolling restless stone,—

FLUELLEN. By your patience, Aunchient Pistol. Fortune is painted blind, with a muffler afore her eyes, to signify to you that Fortune is blind; and she is painted also with a wheel, to signify to you, which is the moral of it, that she is turning, and inconstant, and mutability, and variation: and her foot, look you, is fixed upon a spherical stone, which rolls, and rolls, and rolls: in good truth, the poet makes a most excellent description of it: Fortune is an excellent moral.

PISTOL. Fortune is Bardolph's foe, and frowns on him;
For he hath stolen a pax,[162] and hanged must 'a be:
A damned death!
Let gallows gape for dog; let man go free
And let not hemp his wind-pipe suffocate:
But Exeter hath given the doom of death

---

[161] In the Saxon and our elder English, *buxom* meant *pliant, yielding, obedient;* but it was also used for *lusty, rampant.* Pistol would be more likely to take the popular sense than one founded on etymology.

[162] The *pax* is said to have been a small piece of plate, sometimes with the Crucifixion engraved or embossed upon it, which at a certain point in the Mass was offered to the laity to be kissed: *Osculatorium* was another name for it.

For pax of little price.

Therefore, go speak: the duke will hear thy voice:

And let not Bardolph's vital thread be cut

With edge of penny cord and vile reproach:

Speak, captain, for his life, and I will thee requite.

FLUELLEN. Aunchient Pistol, I do partly understand your meaning.

PISTOL. Why then, rejoice therefore.

FLUELLEN. Certainly, aunchient, it is not a thing to rejoice at: for if, look you, he were my brother, I would desire the duke to use his good pleasure, and put him to execution; for discipline ought to be used.

PISTOL. Die and be damn'd! and *fico* for thy friendship!

FLUELLEN. It is well.

PISTOL. The fig of Spain!¹⁶³ [*Exit.*]

FLUELLEN. Very good.

GOWER. Why, this is an arrant counterfeit rascal; I remember him now; a bawd, a cutpurse.

FLUELLEN. I'll assure you, 'a uttered as brave words at the pridge as you shall see in a summer's day. But it is very well; what he has spoke to me, that is well, I warrant you, when time is serve.

GOWER. Why, 'tis a gull, a fool, a rogue, that now and then goes to the wars, to grace himself at his return into London under the form of a soldier. And such fellows are perfect in the great commanders' names: and they will learn you by rote where services were done; at such and such a sconce,¹⁶⁴ at such a breach, at such a convoy; who came off bravely, who was shot, who disgraced, what terms the enemy stood on; and this they con perfectly in the phrase of war, which they trick up with new-coined oaths: and what a beard of the general's cut,¹⁶⁵ and a horrid suit of the camp will do among foaming bottles and ale-washed wits, is wonderful to be thought on. But you must learn to know such slanders of the age,¹⁶⁶ or else you may be marvellously mistook.

FLUELLEN. I tell you what, Captain Gower; I do perceive he is not the

---

¹⁶³ What is here called "the fig of Spain" was by no means confined to that country, nor did it originate there. It was a coarse gesture of contemptuous insult, made by thrusting the thumb between the middle and fore fingers, so as to form a rude likeness to a certain disease which was called the *ficus* as far back at least as the days of classic Rome.

¹⁶⁴ A *sconce* was a *blockhouse* or *chief fortress*, for the most part round in fashion of a head; hence the head is ludicrously called a sconce; a lantern was also called a sconce, because of its round form.

¹⁶⁵ The English used to be very particular about the *cut* of their beards. Certain ranks and callings had their peculiar style; and soldiers appear to have affected what was called the *spade* cut and the *stiletto* cut.

¹⁶⁶ Nothing was more common than such huffcap pretending braggarts as Pistol in the Poet's age; they are the continual subject of satire to his contemporaries.

man that he would gladly make show to the world he is: if I find a
hole in his coat, I will tell him my mind. [*Drum within.*] Hark you,
the King is coming, and I must speak with him from the
pridge.[167]—

[*Enter* KING HENRY, GLOUCESTER, *and Soldiers.*]

God pless your majesty!
KING HENRY V. How now, Fluellen! camest thou from the pridge?
FLUELLEN. Ay, so please your majesty. The Duke of Exeter has very
gallantly maintained the pridge: the French is gone off, look you;
and there is gallant and most prave passages; marry, th' athversary
was have possession of the pridge; but he is enforced to retire, and
the Duke of Exeter is master of the pridge: I can tell your majesty,
the duke is a prave man.
KING HENRY V. What men have you lost, Fluellen?
FLUELLEN. The perdition of th' athversary hath been very great,
reasonable great: marry, for my part, I think the duke hath lost
never a man, but one that is like to be executed for robbing a
church,—one Bardolph, if your majesty know the man: his face is
all bubukles, and whelks,[168] and knobs, and flames o' fire: and his
lips blows at his nose, and it is like a coal of fire, sometimes plue
and sometimes red; but his nose is executed and his fire's out.
KING HENRY V. We would have all such offenders so cut off: and we
give express charge, that in our marches through the country, there
be nothing compelled from the villages, nothing taken but paid
for,[169] none of the French upbraided or abused in disdainful
language; for when lenity and cruelty play for a kingdom, the
gentler gamester is the soonest winner.

[*Tucket sounds. Enter* MONTJOY.]

MONTJOY. You know me by my habit.[170]
KING HENRY V. Well then I know thee: what shall I know of thee?
MONTJOY. My master's mind.
KING HENRY V. Unfold it.
MONTJOY. Thus says my King: Say thou to Harry of England:
Though we seemed dead, we did but sleep: advantage is a better
soldier than rashness. Tell him we could have rebuked him at

---

[167] "I must tell him what was done at the bridge."

[168] *Bubukles* are blotches or botches; *whelks* are pustules or wheals.

[169] That is, nothing taken *without being* paid for. This use of *but* with the force of *without* occurs repeatedly.

[170] The person of a herald being, by the laws of war, inviolable, was distinguished by a richly-emblazoned dress.

Harfleur, but that we thought not good to bruise an injury till it were full ripe:[171] now we speak upon our cue, and our voice is imperial: England shall repent his folly, see his weakness, and admire our sufferance. Bid him therefore consider of his ransom; which must proportion the losses we have borne, the subjects we have lost, the disgrace we have digested; which in weight to re-answer, his pettiness would bow under. For our losses, his exchequer is too poor; for the effusion of our blood, the muster of his kingdom too faint a number; and for our disgrace, his own person, kneeling at our feet, but a weak and worthless satisfaction. To this add defiance: and tell him, for conclusion, he hath betrayed his followers, whose condemnation is pronounced. So far my King and master; so much my office.

KING HENRY V. What is thy name? I know thy quality.

MONTJOY. Montjoy.

KING HENRY V. Thou dost thy office fairly. Turn thee back.
And tell thy King I do not seek him now;
But could be willing to march on to Calais
Without impeachment:[172] for, to say the sooth,—
Though 'tis no wisdom to confess so much
Unto an enemy of craft and vantage,[173]—
My people are with sickness much enfeebled,
My numbers lessened, and those few I have
Almost no better than so many French;
Who when they were in health, I tell thee, herald,
I thought upon one pair of English legs
Did march three Frenchmen.—Yet, forgive me, God,
That I do brag thus!—this your air of France
Hath blown that vice in me;[174] I must repent.
Go therefore, tell thy master here I am;
My ransom is this frail and worthless trunk,
My army but a weak and sickly guard;
Yet, God before,[175] tell him we will come on,
Though France himself and such another neighbour
Stand in our way. There's for thy labour, Montjoy.

[*Gives a purse.*]

---

[171] The *implied* image is of a sore, as a boil or carbuncle, which is best let alone till it has come to a head.—*Cue* is used in the sense of *turn.*

[172] Without *impediment*; an old use of *impeachment*, now obsolete. Thus in Holinshed: "But the passage was now so *impeached* with stakes in the botome of the foord, that he could not passe."

[173] An enemy both cunning in arts of strategy and having the advantage in ground and numbers.

[174] "Hath *puffed me up* with that vanity."

[175] That is, "God being our guide." See page 11, note 52.

Go bid thy master well advise himself:[176]
If we may pass, we will; if we be hinder'd,
We shall your tawny ground with your red blood
Discolour: and so Montjoy, fare you well.
The sum of all our answer is but this:
We would not seek a battle, as we are;
Nor, as we are, we say we will not shun it:
So tell your master.

MONTJOY. I shall deliver so. Thanks to your highness. [*Exit.*]

GLOUCESTER. I hope they will not come upon us now.

KING HENRY V. We are in God's hand, brother, not in theirs.
March to the pridge; it now draws toward night:
Beyond the river we'll encamp ourselves,
And on to-morrow, bid them march away. [*Exeunt.*]

Scene VI.

The French Camp, near Agincourt.

[*Enter the Constable of France, the Lord* RAMBURES, *the Duke of* ORLEANS, *the* Dauphin, *and others.*]

CONSTABLE. Tut! I have the best armour of the world.—Would it were day!

ORLEANS. You have an excellent armour; but let my horse have his due.

CONSTABLE. It is the best horse of Europe.

ORLEANS. Will it never be morning?

DAUPHIN. My lord of Orleans, and my lord High-Constable, you talk of horse and armour,—

ORLEANS. You are as well provided of both as any prince in the world.

DAUPHIN. What a long night is this!—I will not change my horse with any that treads but on four pasterns. *Ça, ha!* he bounds from the earth, as if his entrails were hairs;[177] *le cheval volant*, the Pegasus, *qui a les narines de feu!* When I bestride him, I soar, I am a hawk: he trots the air; the earth sings when he touches it; the basest horn of his hoof is more musical than the pipe of Hermes.

ORLEANS. He's of the colour of the nutmeg.

DAUPHIN. And of the heat of the ginger. It is a beast for Perseus: he is pure air and fire; and the dull elements of earth and water never appear in him,[178] but only in Patient stillness while his rider

---

[176] *Advise*, again, as before: *bethink* himself, *consider*. Page 11, note 42.

[177] Alluding to the bounding of tennis-balls, which were stuffed with hair.

[178] Alluding to the ancient doctrine that men and animals, as well as other things, were all made up of the four elements, earth, water, air, and fire, and that the higher

mounts him: he is indeed a horse; and all other jades you may call beasts.[179]

CONSTABLE. Indeed, my lord, it is a most absolute and excellent horse.

DAUPHIN. It is the prince of palfreys; his neigh is like the bidding of a monarch and his countenance enforces homage.

ORLEANS. No more, cousin.

DAUPHIN. Nay, the man hath no wit that cannot, from the rising of the lark to the lodging of the lamb, vary deserved praise on my palfrey: it is a theme as fluent as the sea: turn the sands into eloquent tongues, and my horse is argument for them all: 'tis a subject for a sovereign to reason on, and for a sovereign's sovereign to ride on; and for the world, familiar to us and unknown to lay apart their particular functions and wonder at him. I once writ a sonnet in his praise and began thus: *Wonder of nature,—*

ORLEANS. I have heard a sonnet begin so to one's mistress.

DAUPHIN. Then did they imitate that which I composed to my courser, for my horse is my mistress.

ORLEANS. Your mistress bears well.

DAUPHIN. Me well; which is the prescript praise and perfection of a good and particular mistress.

CONSTABLE. Nay, for methought yesterday your mistress shrewdly shook your back.

DAUPHIN. So perhaps did yours.

CONSTABLE. Mine was not bridled.

DAUPHIN. O then belike she was old and gentle; and you rode, like a kern of Ireland, your French hose off, and in your straight strossers.[180]

CONSTABLE. You have good judgment in horsemanship.

DAUPHIN. Be warned by me, then: they that ride so and ride not warily, fall into foul bogs. I had rather have my horse to my mistress.

CONSTABLE. I had as lief have my mistress a jade.

---

natures were rendered so by the preponderance of the two latter in their composition. Thus, in *Antony and Cleopatra*, v. 2, the heroine says, "I am fire and air; my other elements I give to baser life." The Poet has divers allusions to the doctrine.

[179] It appears from this *that jade* and *horse* were sometimes used simply as equivalent terms. On the other hand, *beast* is here meant to convey a note of contempt, like the Latin *jumentum*, as of an animal fit only for the cart or packsaddle.

[180] *Kerns* is equivalent to *boors*, and was used especially of Irish light-armed foot-soldiers.—*Strait strossers* is *tight drawers* or *breeches*. *Strosser* is probably a corruption of *trosser*, another form of *trouser*. So in Middleton's *No Wit, no Help like a Woman's*, ii. 1: "Or, like a toiling usurer, sets his son a-horse-back in cloth-of-gold breeches, while he himself goes to the devil a-foot in a pair of old *strossers*."

DAUPHIN. I tell thee, Constable, my mistress wears his own hair.[181]

CONSTABLE. I could make as true a boast as that, if I had a sow to my mistress.

DAUPHIN. *Le chien est retourné à son propre vomissement, et la truie lavée au bourbier;*[182] thou makest use of any thing.

CONSTABLE. Yet do I not use my horse for my mistress, or any such proverb so little kin to the purpose.

RAMBURES. My lord constable, the armour that I saw in your tent to-night, are those stars or suns upon it?

CONSTABLE. Stars, my lord.

DAUPHIN. Some of them will fall to-morrow, I hope.

CONSTABLE. And yet my sky shall not want.

DAUPHIN. That may be, for you bear a many superfluously, and 'twere more honour some were away.

CONSTABLE. Even as your horse bears your praises; who would trot as well, were some of your brags dismounted.

DAUPHIN. Would I were able to load him with his desert!—Will it never be day?—I will trot to-morrow a mile, and my way shall be paved with English faces.

CONSTABLE. I will not say so, for fear I should be faced out of my way: but I would it were morning; for I would fain be about the ears of the English.

RAMBURES. Who will go to hazard with me for twenty prisoners?

CONSTABLE. You must first go yourself to hazard, ere you have them.

DAUPHIN. 'Tis midnight; I'll go arm myself. [*Exit.*]

ORLEANS. The Dauphin longs for morning.

RAMBURES. He longs to eat the English.

CONSTABLE. I think he will eat all he kills.

ORLEANS. By the white hand of my lady, he's a gallant prince.

CONSTABLE. Swear by her foot, that she may tread out the oath.[183]

ORLEANS. He is simply the most active gentleman of France.

CONSTABLE. Doing is activity; and he will still be doing.[184]

ORLEANS. He never did harm, that I heard of.

CONSTABLE. Nor will do none to-morrow: he will keep that good name still.

ORLEANS. I know him to be valiant.

---

[181] Referring to the custom which some ladies had, as, it is said, some still have, of wearing hair not their own. The Dauphin is jibing and flouting the Constable upon the presumed qualities of the lady whom he calls his mistress.

[182] It has been remarked that Shakespeare was habitually conversant with his Bible: we have here a strong presumptive proof that he read it, at least occasionally, in French. This passage will be found almost literally in the Geneva Bible, 1588. 2 Peter, ii. 22.

[183] To *tread* out an oath is to *dance* it out, probably.

[184] Here, as often, *still* is *continually* or *always.—Doing* is used equivocally, but the poor quibble is not worth comment.

CONSTABLE. I was told that by one that knows him better than you.

ORLEANS. What's he?

CONSTABLE. Marry, he told me so himself; and he said he cared not who knew it.

ORLEANS. He needs not; it is no hidden virtue in him.

CONSTABLE. By my faith, sir, but it is; never any body saw it but his lackey: 'tis a hooded valour; and when it appears, it will bate.[185]

ORLEANS. Ill will never said well.

CONSTABLE. I will cap that proverb with—There is flattery in friendship.

ORLEANS. And I will take up that with—Give the devil his due.

CONSTABLE. Well placed: there stands your friend for the devil: have at the very eye of that proverb with—A pox of the Devil.

ORLEANS. You are the better at proverbs, by how much—A fool's bolt[186] is soon shot.

CONSTABLE. You have shot over.

ORLEANS. 'Tis not the first time you were overshot.[187]

[*Enter a* MESSENGER.]

MESSENGER. My lord High-Constable, the English lie within fifteen hundred paces of your tents.

CONSTABLE. Who hath measured the ground?

MESSENGER. The Lord Grandpre.

CONSTABLE. A valiant and most expert gentleman. Would it were day! Alas, poor Harry of England! he longs not for the dawning as we do.

ORLEANS. What a wretched and peevish[188] fellow is this King of England, to mope with his fat-brained followers so far out of his knowledge!

CONSTABLE. If the English had any apprehension,[189] they would run away.

ORLEANS. That they lack; for if their heads had any intellectual

---

[185] This pun depends upon the equivocal use of *bate*. When a hawk is unhooded, her first action is to bate, that is, beat her wings, or flutter. The Constable would insinuate that the Dauphin's courage, when he prepares for encounter, will *bate*, that is, soon diminish or evaporate. *Hooded* is *blindfolded*.

[186] A *bolt* was a short, thick, blunt arrow, for shooting near objects, and so requiring little or no skill.

[187] *Overshot*, here, probably means *disgraced* or *put to shame*; though one of its meanings is *intoxicated*.

[188] *Peevish* was often used in the sense of *mad or foolish*. So in *The Comedy of Errors*, iv. 1: "How now! a *madman*? why, thou *peevish* sheep, what ship of Epidamnum stays for me?"—To *mope* is to move or act *languidly* or *drowsily*, or as in a half-conscious state.—The Poet uses *fat-brain'd* and *fat-witted* for *dull* or *stupid*.

[189] *Apprehension* for *mental quickness, intelligence,* or aptness to perceive; as to *apprehend* is, properly, to *grasp, seize,* or *lay hold of.*

armour, they could never wear such heavy head-pieces.

RAMBURES. That island of England breeds very valiant creatures; their mastiffs are of unmatchable courage.

ORLEANS. Foolish curs, that run winking into the mouth of a Russian bear and have their heads crushed like rotten apples! You may as well say, that's a valiant flea that dare eat his breakfast on the lip of a lion.

CONSTABLE. Just, just; and the men do sympathize with the mastiffs in robustious and rough coming on, leaving their wits with their wives: and then give them great meals of beef and iron and steel, they will eat like wolves and fight like devils.

ORLEANS. Ay, but these English are shrewdly out of beef.

CONSTABLE. Then shall we find to-morrow they have only stomachs to eat and none to fight. Now is it time to arm: come, shall we about it?

ORLEANS. It is now two o'clock: but, let me see,—by ten
We shall have each a hundred Englishmen. [*Exeunt.*]

ACT IV.

[*Enter* CHORUS.]

CHORUS. Now entertain conjecture of a time
    When creeping murmur and the poring[190] dark
    Fills the wide vessel of the universe.
    From camp to camp through the foul womb of night
    The hum of either army stilly sounds,
    That the fixed sentinels[191] almost receive
    The secret whispers of each other's watch:
    Fire answers fire, and through their paly flames
    Each battle sees the other's umber'd[192] face;
    Steed threatens steed, in high and boastful neighs
    Piercing the night's dull ear, and from the tents
    The armourers, accomplishing the knights,
    With busy hammers closing rivets up,[193]

---

[190] To *pore* is to look intently, needfully, or with strained vision; and *poring* is here, no doubt, an instance of what is called transferred epithet: the darkness in which we look as aforesaid, or *grope*.

[191] That is, the sentinels *stationed*, or remaining at their posts.—*That* has the force of *so that*; a very frequent usage.

[192] It has been said that the distant visages of the soldiers would appear of an *umber* colour when beheld through the light of midnight fires. I suspect that nothing more is meant than *shadow'd face*. The epithet *paly flames* is against the other interpretation. *Umbre* for *shadow* is common in our elder writers.

[193] This does not solely refer to the riveting the plate armour before it was put on, but also to a part when it was on. The top of the cuirass had a little projecting bit of iron

Give dreadful note of preparation:
The country cocks do crow, the clocks do toll,
And the third hour of drowsy morning name.
Proud of their numbers and secure in soul,
The confident and over-lusty French
Do the low-rated English play at dice;[194]
And chide the cripple tardy-gaited night
Who, like a foul and ugly witch, doth limp
So tediously away. The poor condemned English,
Like sacrifices, by their watchful fires
Sit patiently and inly ruminate
The morning's danger, and their gesture sad
Investing lank-lean; cheeks,[195] and war-worn coats
Presenteth them unto the gazing moon
So many horrid ghosts. O now, who will behold
The royal captain of this ruin'd band
Walking from watch to watch, from tent to tent,
Let him cry, *Praise and glory on his head*!
For forth he goes and visits all his host.
Bids them good morrow with a modest smile
And calls them brothers, friends and countrymen.
Upon his royal face there is no note
How dread an army hath enrounded him;
Nor doth he dedicate one jot of colour
Unto the weary and all-watched night,
But freshly looks and over-bears attaint[196]
With cheerful semblance and sweet majesty;
That every wretch, pining and pale before,
Beholding him, plucks comfort from his looks:
A largess universal like the sun

---

that passed through a hole in the bottom of the casque. When both were put on, the armourer presented himself, with his riveting hammer, *to* close *the rivet up.*

[194] The Poet took this from Holinshed: "The Frenchmen in the meane while, as though they had beene sure of victorie, made great triumph; for the capteins had determined how to divide the spoile, and the soldiers the night before had plaid the Englishmen at dice."

[195] The metaphor of a gesture *investing* cheeks seems rather harsh and strained. But *gesture*, in the sense of the Latin original, may very well be used of a look, or any form of expression addressed to the eye. And to speak of a *look* as *overspreading* or *covering* the face, is legitimate enough. We have a like figure in *Much Ado*, iv. 1: "I am so *attired* in wonder." Also, in Sidney's Astrophel: "Anger *invests* the face with a lovely grace."— Perhaps it should be added that *and* connects *coats* to *gesture*, not to *cheeks*: "and *their* war-worn coats."

[196] *Attaint*, or *taint*, was often used for *attainture* or *attainder*, in the sense *of impeachment* or *accusation*. The meaning is, that the King by his brave and cheerful look overcomes all disposition on the part of the soldiers to blame or reproach him for the plight they are in.

His liberal eye doth give to every one,
Thawing cold fear, that mean and gentle all,
Behold, as may unworthiness define,
A little touch of Harry in the night.[197]
And so our scene must to the battle fly;
Where—O for pity!—we shall much disgrace
With four or five most vile and ragged foils,
Right ill-disposed in brawl ridiculous,
The name of Agincourt. Yet sit and see,
Minding[198] true things by what their mockeries be. [*Exit.*]

SCENE I.

France. The English Camp at Agincourt.

[*Enter* KING HENRY, BEDFORD, *and* GLOUCESTER.]

KING HENRY V. Gloucester, 'tis true that we are in great danger;
    The greater therefore should our courage be.—
    Good morrow, brother Bedford.—God Almighty!
    There is some soul of goodness in things evil,
    Would men observingly distil it out.
    For our bad neighbour makes us early stirrers,
    Which is both healthful and good husbandry:
    Besides, they are our outward consciences,
    And preachers to us all, admonishing
    That we should 'dress[199] us fairly for our end.
    Thus may we gather honey from the weed,
    And make a moral of the devil himself.—

[*Enter* ERPINGHAM.]

Good morrow, old Sir Thomas Erpingham:
A good soft pillow for that good white head
Were better than a churlish turf of France.
ERPINGHAM. Not so, my liege: this lodging likes me better,
    Since I may say *Now lie I like a King.*
KING HENRY V. 'Tis good for men to love their present pains
    Upon example; so the spirit is eased:
    And when the mind is quicken'd, out of doubt,

---

[197] The meaning, as I take it, is, "so that, to describe the thing inadequately, men of all ranks in the army get a little glimpse or taste of Harry in the night."

[198] *Minding,* here, is the same as *calling to mind.*

[199] Here '*dress* is a contraction of *address,* which the Poet often uses for *make ready* or *prepare.* So in *Macbeth,* i. 7: "Was the hope drunk wherein you '*dress'd* yourself?"

The organs, though defunct and dead before,
Break up their drowsy grave and newly move,
With casted slough and fresh legerity.[200]
Lend me thy cloak, Sir Thomas.—Brothers both,
Commend me to the princes in our camp;
Do my good morrow to them, and anon
Desire them an to my pavilion.
GLOUCESTER. We shall, my liege.
BEDFORD. Shall I attend your grace?
KING HENRY V. No, my good knight;
   Go with my brothers to my lords of England:
   I and my bosom must debate awhile,
   And then I would no other company.
ERPINGHAM. The Lord in heaven bless thee, noble Harry!

   [*Exeunt* GLOUCESTER, BEDFORD, *and* ERPINGHAM.]

KING HENRY V. God-a-mercy, old heart! thou speak'st cheerfully.

   [*Enter* PISTOL.]

PISTOL. *Qui va là?*
KING HENRY V. A friend.
PISTOL. Discuss unto me; art thou officer?
   Or art thou base, common and popular?
KING HENRY V. I am a gentleman of a company.
PISTOL. Trail'st thou the puissant pike?
KING HENRY V. Even so. What are you?
PISTOL. As good a gentleman as the emperor.
KING HENRY V. Then you are a better than the King.
PISTOL. The King's a bawcock, and a heart of gold,
   A lad of life, an imp[201] of fame;
   Of parents good, of fist most valiant.
   I kiss his dirty shoe, and from heart-string
   I love the lovely bully. What is thy name?
KING HENRY V. Harry *le Roi*.
PISTOL. Le Roy!
   A Cornish name: art thou of Cornish crew?
KING HENRY V. No, I am a Welshman.[202]

---

[200] The allusion is to the casting of the *slough* or skin of the snake annually, by which act he is supposed to regain new vigour and fresh youth. *Legerity* is lightness, nimbleness. *Légèreté*, French.

[201] The original meaning of *imp* is *graff, scion,* or *sprout.*

[202] He calls himself a Welshman because he was in fact born at Monmouth in Wales. Hence his surname, Harry of *Monmouth.*

PISTOL. Know'st thou Fluellen?

KING HENRY V. Yes.

PISTOL. Tell him, I'll knock his leek about his pate
    Upon Saint Davy's day.[203]

KING HENRY V. Do not you wear your dagger in your cap that day,
    lest he knock that about yours.

PISTOL. Art thou his friend?

KING HENRY V. And his kinsman too.

PISTOL. The *fico* for thee, then!

KING HENRY V. I thank you: God be with you!

PISTOL. My name is Pistol call'd. [*Exit.*]

KING HENRY V. It sorts well with your fierceness.

[*Enter* FLUELLEN *and* GOWER, *severally.*]

GOWER. Captain Fluellen!

FLUELLEN. So! in the name of Jesu Christ, speak lower. It is the
    greatest admiration[204] of the universal world, when the true and
    aunchient prerogatifes and laws of the wars is not kept: if you
    would take the pains but to examine the wars of Pompey the Great,
    you shall find, I warrant you, that there is no tiddle-taddle nor
    pibble-pabble in Pompey's camp; I warrant you, you shall find the
    ceremonies of the wars, and the cares of it, and the forms of it, and
    the sobriety of it, and the modesty of it, to be otherwise.

GOWER. Why, the enemy is loud; you hear him all night.

FLUELLEN. If the enemy is an ass and a fool and a prating coxcomb,
    is it meet, think you, that we should also, look you, be an ass and a
    fool and a prating coxcomb,—in your own conscience, now?

GOWER. I will speak lower.

FLUELLEN. I pray you and beseech you that you will.

[*Exeunt* GOWER *and* FLUELLEN.]

KING HENRY V. Though it appear a little out of fashion,
    There is much care and valour in this Welshman.

[*Enter* BATES, COURT, *and* WILLIAMS.]

COURT. Brother John Bates, is not that the morning which breaks
    yonder?

BATES. I think it be: but we have no great cause to desire the approach

---

[203] Saint David is the patron saint of Wales, and of course his day stands high in the Welsh calendar; a national holiday.

[204] *Admiration*, as usual, in the Latin sense of *wonder*.

of day.

WILLIAMS. We see yonder the beginning of the day, but I think we shall never see the end of it.—Who goes there?

KING HENRY V. A friend.

WILLIAMS. Under what captain serve you?

KING HENRY V. Under Sir Thomas Erpingham.

WILLIAMS. A good old commander and a most kind gentleman: I pray you, what thinks he of our estate?[205]

KING HENRY V. Even as men wrecked upon a sand, that look to be washed off the next tide.

BATES. He hath not told his thought to the King?

KING HENRY V. No; nor it is not meet he should. For, though I speak it to you, I think the King is but a man, as I am: the violet smells to him as it doth to me: the element[206] shows to him as it doth to me; all his senses have but human conditions: his ceremonies laid by, in his nakedness he appears but a man; and though his affections are higher mounted than ours, yet, when they stoop, they stoop with the like wing.[207] Therefore when he sees reason of fears, as we do, his fears, out of doubt, be of the same relish as ours are: yet, in reason, no man should possess him with any appearance of fear, lest he, by showing it, should dishearten his army.

BATES. He may show what outward courage he will; but I believe, as cold a night as 'tis, he could wish himself in Thames up to the neck; and so I would he were, and I by him, at all adventures, so we were quit here.

KING HENRY V. By my troth, I will speak my conscience of the King: I think he would not wish himself any where but where he is.

BATES. Then I would he were here alone; so should he be sure to be ransomed, and a many poor men's lives saved.

KING HENRY V. I dare say you love him not so ill, to wish him here alone, howsoever you speak this to feel other men's minds: methinks I could not die any where so contented as in the King's company; his cause being just and his quarrel honourable.

WILLIAMS. That's more than we know.

BATES. Ay, or more than we should seek after; for we know enough, if we know we are the kings subjects: if his cause be wrong, our obedience to the King wipes the crime of it out of us.

WILLIAMS. But if the cause be not good, the King himself hath a heavy reckoning to make, when all those legs and arms and heads,

---

[205] *Estate* and *state* were used indiscriminately.

[206] The *element* is the *sky*. Repeatedly so.

[207] An allusion to falconry. When a hawk, after soaring or mounting aloft, took his flight downwards, he was said to *stoop*: especially used of the plunge or *souse* he made upon the prey.—"Higher mounted" is *soaring* to a higher pitch; another instance of the confusion of active and passive forms.

chopped off in battle, shall join together at the latter day and cry all *We died at such a place*; some swearing, some crying for a surgeon, some upon their wives left poor behind them, some upon the debts they owe, some upon their children rawly left.[208] I am afeard there are few die well that die in a battle; for how can they charitably dispose of any thing, when blood is their argument?[209] Now, if these men do not die well, it will be a black matter for the King that led them to it; whom to disobey were against all proportion of subjection.

KING HENRY V. So, if a son that is by his father sent about merchandise do sinfully miscarry upon the sea, the imputation of his wickedness by your rule, should be imposed upon his father that sent him: or if a servant, under his master's command transporting a sum of money, be assailed by robbers and die in many irreconciled iniquities,[210] you may call the business of the master the author of the servant's damnation: but this is not so: the King is not bound to answer the particular endings of his soldiers, the father of his son, nor the master of his servant; for they purpose not their death, when they purpose their services. Besides, there is no King, be his cause never so spotless, if it come to the arbitrement of swords, can try it out with all unspotted soldiers: some peradventure have on them the guilt of premeditated and contrived murder; some, of beguiling virgins with the broken seals of perjury;[211] some, making the wars their bulwark, that have before gored the gentle bosom of peace with pillage and robbery. Now, if these men have defeated the law and outrun native punishment,[212] though they can outstrip men, they have no wings to fly from God: war is his beadle, war is vengeance; so that here men are punished for before-breach of the King's laws in now the King's quarrel: where they feared the death, they have borne life away; and where they would be safe, they perish: then if they die unprovided, no more is the King guilty of their damnation than he was before guilty of those impieties for the which they are now visited. Every subject's duty is the King's; but every subject's soul is his own. Therefore should every soldier in the wars do as every sick man in his bed,—wash every mote out of his conscience: and

---

[208] Their children left young and helpless; in a *raw* or *green age*.

[209] *Argument*, in Shakespeare, is *theme, subject, purpose*, any matter in thought, or any business in hand.—"Charitably dispose" alludes to the old doctrine that a Christian's last hours should be spent in making such provision as he can for the poor and needy and suffering human brethren whom he is leaving behind.

[210] The language is slightly elliptical: iniquities for which he has not made his peace with Heaven by repentance and restitution.

[211] "The broken seals of perjury" are the *seals* or *vows* broken by perjury.

[212] "*Native* punishment" probably means punishment *at home*, or the punishment ordained in or by their native land.

dying so, death is to him advantage; or not dying, the time was blessedly lost wherein such preparation was gained: and in him that escapes, it were not sin to think that, making God so free an offer, He let him outlive that day to see His greatness and to teach others how they should prepare.

WILLIAMS. 'Tis certain, every man that dies ill, the ill upon his own head, the King is not to answer it.

BATES. But I do not desire he should answer for me; and yet I determine to fight lustily for him.

KING HENRY V. I myself heard the King say he would not be ransomed.

WILLIAMS. Ay, he said so, to make us fight cheerfully: but when our throats are cut, he may be ransomed, and we ne'er the wiser.

KING HENRY V. If I live to see it, I will never trust his word after.

WILLIAMS. 'Mass, you pay[213] him then. That's a perilous shot out of an elder-gun, that a poor and private displeasure can do against a monarch! you may as well go about to turn the sun to ice with fanning in his face with a peacock's feather. You'll never trust his word after! come, 'tis a foolish saying.

KING HENRY V. Your reproof is something too round:[214] I should be angry with you, if the time were convenient.

WILLIAMS. Let it be a quarrel between us, if you live.

KING HENRY V. I embrace it.

WILLIAMS. How shall I know thee again?

KING HENRY V. Give me any gage of thine, and I will wear it in my bonnet:[215] then, if ever thou darest acknowledge it, I will make it my quarrel.

WILLIAMS. Here's my glove: give me another of thine.

KING HENRY V. There.

WILLIAMS. This will I also wear in my cap: if ever thou come to me and say, after to-morrow, *This is my glove*, by this hand, I will take thee a box on the ear.

KING HENRY V. If ever I live to see it, I will challenge it.

WILLIAMS. Thou darest as well be hanged.

KING HENRY V. Well. I will do it, though I take thee in the King's company.

WILLIAMS. Keep thy word: fare thee well.

BATES. Be friends, you English fools, be friends: we have French quarrels enow, if you could tell how to reckon.

KING HENRY V. Indeed, the French may lay twenty French crowns to

---

[213] *Pay* here means *bring him to account*, or *requite his act.*—An *elder-gun* is a *popgun*; so called because made by punching the pith out of a piece of elder.

[214] *Round* is *plain-spoken, unceremonious, blunt.* Often so.

[215] *Bonnet* was the common name of a man's head-covering.—*Gage* is *pledge*, that which proves an *engagement.*

one, they will beat us; for they bear them on their shoulders: but it
is no English treason to cut French crowns, and to-morrow the
King himself will be a clipper.[216]—

[*Exeunt soldiers.*]

Upon the King! let us our lives, our souls,
Our debts, our careful wives,[217] our children and
Our sins lay on the King! We must bear all.
O hard condition, twin-born with greatness,
Subject to the breath of every fool, whose sense
No more can feel but his own wringing![218]
What infinite heart's-ease must kings neglect,
That private men enjoy!
And what have kings, that privates have not too,
Save ceremony,—save general ceremony?—
And what art thou, thou idle ceremony?
What kind of god art thou, that suffer'st more
Of mortal griefs than do thy worshippers?
What are thy rents? what are thy comings in?
O ceremony, show me but thy worth!
What is thy soul of adoration?[219]
Art thou aught else but place, degree and form,
Creating awe and fear in other men?
Wherein thou art less happy being fear'd
Than they in fearing.
What drink'st thou oft, instead of homage sweet,
But poison'd flattery? O, be sick, great greatness,
And bid thy ceremony give thee cure!
Think'st thou the fiery fever will go out
With titles blown from adulation?[220]
Will it give place to flexure and low bending?
Canst thou, when thou command'st the beggar's knee,
Command the health of it? No, thou proud dream,

---

[216] Alluding to the old doctrine which made it treason to mar or deface the king's image on the coin. There is a quibble also on *crowns*; the King probably meaning that there are twenty Frenchmen to one Englishman.

[217] "Our careful wives" probably means "the wives whom we care, or are careful, for." Another instance of transferred epithet. See page 11, note 190.

[218] Who has no sense or feeling for any pains or troubles but his own: without sympathy; uncompassionate; and therefore selfish. To *wring* and to *writhe* have the same meaning. So in *Cymbeline*, iii. 6: "He *wrings* at some distress."

[219] Such was the idiom of the time; the sense being, "What is the life, virtue, or essence of thy adoration?" that is, the adoration paid to thee. The objective genitive, as it is called, where present usage admits only the subjective.

[220] That is, titles blown up, or made big and pretentious with the breath of flattery.

That play'st so subtly with a King's repose;
I am a King that find thee, and I know
'Tis not the balm,[221] the sceptre and the ball,
The sword, the mace, the crown imperial,
The intertissued robe of gold and pearl,
The farcèd[222] title running 'fore the *King*,
The throne he sits on, nor the tide of pomp
That beats upon the high shore of this world,—
No, not all these, thrice-gorgeous ceremony,
Not all these, laid in bed majestical,
Can sleep so soundly as the wretched slave,
Who with a body fill'd and vacant mind
Gets him to rest, cramm'd with distressful[223] bread;
Never sees horrid night, the child of hell,
But, like a lackey, from the rise to set
Sweats in the eye of Phoebus and all night
Sleeps in Elysium; next day after dawn,
Doth rise and help Hyperion to his horse;[224]
And follows so the ever-running year,
With profitable labour, to his grave:
And, but for ceremony, such a wretch,
Winding up days with toil and nights with sleep,
Had the fore-hand and vantage of a King.
The slave, a member of the country's peace,
Enjoys it; but in gross brain little wots
What watch the King keeps to maintain the peace,
Whose hours the peasant best advantages.[225]

[*Enter* ERPINGHAM.]

ERPINGHAM. My lord, your nobles, jealous of your absence,
  Seek through your camp to find you.
KING HENRY V. Good old knight,
  Collect them all together at my tent:

---

[221] The *balm* was the oil used in anointing a king at his coronation.—The ball was the symbol of *majesty*; the mace, of *authority*.

[222] Farced is *stuffed*. The tumid, puffy titles with which a king's name is introduced.

[223] Distressful, perhaps, in a twofold sense: the poor man is distressed to get it, and distressed after eating it.

[224] *Horse'* for *horses*, just as, elsewhere, *corpse'* for *corpses*, and *house'* for *houses*: for the old Sun-god, whether called Hyperion, Apollo, or Phœbus, was never a one-horse god; nor could his grand chariot be drawn by a one-horse team; and Shakespeare knew this right well.

[225] In the old writers, the predicate verb often agrees in number with the nearest substantive, and not with the proper subject. So here, *hours* is the subject of *advantages*, which is a transitive verb, *peasant* being its object.

I'll be before thee.
ERPINGHAM. I shall do't, my lord. [*Exit.*]
KING HENRY V. O God of battles! steel my soldiers' hearts;
    Possess them not with fear; take from them now
    The sense of reckoning, if the opposed numbers
    Pluck their hearts from them. Not to-day, O Lord,
    O, not to-day, think not upon the fault
    My father made in compassing the crown!
    I Richard's body have interred anew;
    And on it have bestow'd more contrite tears
    Than from it issued forced drops of blood:
    Five hundred poor I have in yearly pay,
    Who twice a-day their wither'd hands hold up
    Toward heaven, to pardon blood; and I have built
    Two chantries,[226] where the sad and solemn priests
    Sing still for Richard's soul. More will I do;
    Though all that I can do is nothing worth,
    Since that my penitence comes after all,
    Imploring pardon.[227]

[*Enter* GLOUCESTER.]

GLOUCESTER. My liege!
KING HENRY V. My brother Gloucester's voice? Ay;
    I know thy errand, I will go with thee:
    The day, my friends and all things stay for me. [*Exeunt.*]

SCENE II.

The French camp.

[*Enter the* Dauphin, ORLEANS, RAMBURES, *and others.*]

ORLEANS. The sun doth gild our armour; up, my lords!
DAUPHIN. *Montez à cheval!*—My horse! *varlet! laquais!* ha!
ORLEANS. O brave spirit!
DAUPHIN. *Via!*[228]—*les eaux et la terre,*—

---

    [226] One of these was for Carthusian monks, and was called *Bethlehem*; the other was for religious men and women of the order of St. Bridget, and was named *Sion.* They were on opposite sides of the Thames, and adjoined the royal manor of Sheen. A *chantry* is, properly, a place where *chanting* is practised; or a chapel for choral service.
    [227] That is, "Since, after all that I have done or can do in works of piety and charity, nothing but true penitence and earnest prayer for pardon will avail to procure a remission of my sins."
    [228] An old exclamation of encouragement; *on! away!* Italian.

ORLEANS. *Rien puis*? *L'air et la feu,*—
DAUPHIN. *Ciel*! cousin Orleans.

[*Enter* CONSTABLE.]

Now, my lord constable!
CONSTABLE. Hark, how our steeds for present service neigh!
DAUPHIN. Mount them, and make incision in their hides,
    That their hot blood may spin in English eyes,
    And dout them[229] with superfluous courage, ha!
RAMBURES. What, will you have them weep our horses' blood?
    How shall we, then, behold their natural tears?

[*Enter* MESSENGER.]

MESSENGER. The English are embattled, you French peers.
CONSTABLE. To horse, you gallant princes! straight to horse!
    Do but behold yon poor and starved band,
    And your fair show shall suck away their souls,
    Leaving them but the shales[230] and husks of men.
    There is not work enough for all our hands;
    Scarce blood enough in all their sickly veins
    To give each naked curtle-axe a stain,
    That our French gallants shall to-day draw out,
    And sheathe for lack of sport: let us but blow on them,
    The vapour of our valour will o'erturn them.
    'Tis positive 'gainst all exceptions, lords,
    That our superfluous lackeys and our peasants—
    Who in unnecessary action swarm
    About our squares of battle—were enough
    To purge this field of such a hilding foe;[231]
    Though we upon this mountain's basis by
    Took stand for idle speculation,[232]—
    But that our honours must not. What's to say?
    A very little little let us do.
    And all is done. Then let the trumpets sound
    The tucket sonance and the note to mount:[233]

---

[229] To *dout* is to *do out*, to *put out*; *them* referring to *eyes*.

[230] *Shale* is an old form of *shell*; from the Saxon *schale*.

[231] A *hilding* foe is a paltry, cowardly, base foe.

[232] *Speculation*, here, is simply *beholding*, or *looking on*.

[233] The *tucket-sonance*, or *sounding* of the *tucket*, was a flourish on a trumpet as a
signal.—The Constable's spirits are dancing in merry scorn; *the note to mount* and *dare
the field* being terms fitter for a sporting-excursion than for a war-tussle. To *dare the field*
is a phrase in falconry. Birds are *dared* when, by the falcon in the air, they are terrified
from rising, so as to be sometimes taken by the hand.

For our approach shall so much dare the field
That England shall couch down in fear and yield.

[*Enter* GRANDPRE.]

GRANDPRE. Why do you stay so long, my lords of France?
    Yon island carrions, desperate of their bones,
    Ill-favouredly become the morning field:
    Their ragged curtains[234] poorly are let loose,
    And our air shakes them passing scornfully;
    Big Mars seems bankrupt in their beggar'd host
    And faintly through a rusty beaver[235] peeps:
    The horsemen sit like fixed candlesticks,[236]
    With torch-staves in their hand; and their poor jades
    Lob down their heads, dropping the hides and hips,
    The gum down-roping from their pale-dead eyes
    And in their pale dull mouths the gimmal-bit[237]
    Lies foul with chew'd grass, still and motionless;
    And their executors, the knavish crows,
    Fly o'er them, all impatient for their hour.
    Description cannot suit itself in words
    To demonstrate the life of such a battle
    In life so lifeless as it shows itself.
CONSTABLE. They have said their prayers, and they stay for death.
DAUPHIN. Shall we go send them dinners and fresh suits
    And give their fasting horses provender,
    And after fight with them?
CONSTABLE. I stay but for my guidon: to the field!
    I will the banner from a trumpet[238] take,
    And use it for my haste. Come, come, away!
    The sun is high, and we outwear the day. [*Exeunt.*]

---

[234] Their ragged *curtains* are their *colours.*

[235] The *beaver* was the part of the helmet that came down over the face.

[236] Ancient candlesticks were often in the form of human figures holding the socket, for the lights, in their extended hands.

[237] The *gimmal-bit* was probably a bit in which two parts or links were united, as in the *gimmal* ring, so called because they were double-linked; *from gemellus*, Lat.

[238] *Trumpet* for *trumpeter*; a frequent usage.—*Guidon* is an old word for *standard, ensign*, or *banner*, or the *bearer* of it. So Holinshed: "They thought themselves so sure of victorie, that diverse of the noblemen made such hast toward the battell, that they left manie of their servants and *men of warre* behind them, and some of them would not once *staie for their standards*; as amongst other the duke of Brabant, when his *standard* was not come, caused a *banner to be taken from a trumpet*, and fastened to a speare, the which he commanded to be borne before him, instead of his standard."

SCENE III.

The English Camp.

[*Enter the English Host*; GLOUCESTER, BEDFORD, EXETER,
ERPINGHAM, SALISBURY *and* WESTMORELAND.]

GLOUCESTER. Where is the King?
BEDFORD. The King himself is rode to view their battle.
WESTMORELAND. Of fighting men they have full three score
    thousand.
EXETER. There's five to one; besides, they all are fresh.
SALISBURY. God's arm strike with us! 'tis a fearful odds.
    God be wi' you, princes all; I'll to my charge:
    If we no more meet till we meet in heaven,
    Then, joyfully, my noble Lord of Bedford,
    My dear Lord Gloucester, and my good Lord Exeter,
    And my kind kinsman,[239] warriors all, adieu!
BEDFORD. Farewell, good Salisbury; and good luck go with thee!
EXETER. Farewell, kind lord; fight valiantly to-day:
    And yet I do thee wrong to mind thee of it,
    For thou art framed of the firm truth of valour.

    [*Exit* SALISBURY.]

BEDFORD. He is full of valour as of kindness;
    Princely in both.

    [*Enter* KING HENRY V.]

WESTMORELAND. O that we now had here
    But one ten thousand of those men in England
    That do no work to-day!
KING HENRY V. What's he that wishes so?
    My cousin Westmoreland?—No, my fair cousin:[240]
    If we are mark'd to die, we are enow
    To do our country loss; and if to live,

---

[239] The kind kinsman here addressed is Westmoreland. The Earl of Salisbury was Thomas Montacute: he was in fact not related to Westmoreland; but their families were connected by marriage.

[240] Westmoreland's first wife was aunt to the King by his grandfather's side; she being one of several children of John of Ghent by Catharine Swynford; all born out of wedlock, but afterwards legitimated. They took the name of Beaufort, from Beaufort Castle, in France, where they were born.

The fewer men, the greater share of honour.
God's will! I pray thee, wish not one man more.
By Jove, I am not covetous for gold,
Nor care I who doth feed upon my cost;
It yearns me not if men my garments wear;
Such outward things dwell not in my desires:
But if it be a sin to covet honour,
I am the most offending soul alive.
No, faith, my coz, wish not a man from England:
God's peace! I would not lose so great an honour
As one man more, methinks, would share from me
For the best hope I have. O, do not wish one more!
Rather proclaim it, Westmoreland, through my host,
That he which hath no stomach to this fight,
Let him depart; his passport shall be made
And crowns for convoy put into his purse:
We would not die in that man's company
That fears his fellowship to die with us.
This day is called the feast of Crispian:[241]
He that outlives this day, and comes safe home,
Will stand a tip-toe when the day is named,
And rouse him at the name of Crispian.
He that shall live this day, and see old age,
Will yearly on the vigil[242] feast his neighbours,
And say *To-morrow is Saint Crispian*:
Then will he strip his sleeve and show his scars.
And say *These wounds I had on Crispin's day*.
Old men forget: yet all shall be forgot,
But he'll remember with advantages
What feats he did that day: then shall our names.
Familiar in his mouth as household words,—
Harry the King, Bedford and Exeter,
Warwick and Talbot, Salisbury and Gloucester,—
Be in their flowing cups freshly remember'd.
This story shall the good man teach his son;
And Crispin Crispian shall ne'er go by,
From this day to the ending of the world,

---

[241] The battle of Agincourt was fought the 25th of October, 1415. The saints who gave name to the day were Crispin and Crispianus, brothers, born at Rome, from whence they travelled to Soissons, in France, about the year 303, to propagate Christianity, but, that they might not be chargeable to others for their maintenance, they exercised the trade of shoemakers: the governor of the town, discovering them to be Christians, ordered them to be beheaded. Hence they have become the patron saints of shoemakers.

[242] The *vigil of* a holy day was the watch that was kept the night before. Something of the old custom survives in the celebration of Christmas *eve*.

But we in it shall be remember'd;
We few, we happy few, we band of brothers;
For he to-day that sheds his blood with me
Shall be my brother; be he ne'er so vile,
This day shall gentle his condition:[243]
And gentlemen in England now a-bed
Shall think themselves accursed they were not here,
And hold their manhoods cheap whiles any speaks
That fought with us upon Saint Crispin's day.

[*Re-enter* SALISBURY.]

SALISBURY. My sovereign lord, bestow yourself with speed:
  The French are bravely[244] in their battles set,
  And will with all expedience[245] charge on us.
KING HENRY V. All things are ready, if our minds be so.
WESTMORELAND. Perish the man whose mind is backward now!
KING HENRY V. Thou dost not wish more help from England, coz?
WESTMORELAND. God's will! my liege, would you and I alone,
  Without more help, could fight this royal battle!
KING HENRY V. Why, now thou hast unwish'd five thousand men;[246]
  Which likes me better than to wish us one.—
  You know your places: God be with you all!

[*Tucket. Enter* MONTJOY.]

MONTJOY. Once more I come to know of thee, King Harry,
  If for thy ransom thou wilt now compound,
  Before thy most assured overthrow:
  For certainly thou art so near the gulf,
  Thou needs must be englutted. Besides, in mercy,
  The constable desires thee thou wilt mind
  Thy followers of repentance; that their souls
  May make a peaceful and a sweet retire
  From off these fields, where, wretches, their poor bodies
  Must lie and fester.

---

[243] That is, shall make him a gentleman. King Henry V. inhibited any person, but such as had a right by inheritance or grant, from bearing coats-of-arms, except those who fought with him at the battle of Agincourt.

[244] *Bravely* is *in a braving manner*; defiantly.

[245] *Expedience* for *expedition, speed.* The usage was common.

[246] "By wishing only thyself and me, thou hast wished five thousand men away." The Poet, inattentive to numbers, puts five *thousand,* but in the last scene the French are said to be full three-score *thousand,* which Exeter declares to be five to one. The numbers of the English are variously stated; Holinshed makes them fifteen thousand, others but nine thousand.

KING HENRY V. Who hath sent thee now?
MONTJOY. The Constable of France.
KING HENRY V. I pray thee, bear my former answer back:
    Bid them achieve me and then sell my bones.
    Good God! why should they mock poor fellows thus?
    The man that once did sell the lion's skin
    While the beast lived, was killed with hunting him.
    A many of our bodies shall no doubt
    Find native graves; upon the which, I trust,
    Shall witness live in brass[247] of this day's work:
    And those that leave their valiant bones in France,
    Dying like men, though buried in your dunghills,
    They shall be famed; for there the sun shall greet them,
    And draw their honours reeking up to heaven;
    Leaving their earthly parts to choke your clime,
    The smell whereof shall breed a plague in France.
    Mark then abounding valour in our English,
    That being dead, like to the bullet's grazing,
    Break out into a second course of mischief,
    Killing in relapse of mortality.[248]
    Let me speak proudly: tell the constable
    We are but warriors for the working-day;
    Our gayness and our gilt are all besmirch'd
    With rainy marching in the painful field;
    There's not a piece of feather in our host,—
    Good argument, I hope, we will not fly,—
    And time hath worn us into slovenry:
    But, by the mass, our hearts are in the trim;
    And my poor soldiers tell me, yet ere night
    They'll be in fresher robes, or they will pluck
    The gay new coats o'er the French soldiers' heads
    And turn them out of service. If they do this,—
    As, if God please, they shall,—my ransom then
    Will soon be levied. Herald, save thou thy labour;
    Come thou no more for ransom, gentle herald:
    They shall have none, I swear, but these my joints;
    Which if they have as I will leave 'em them,
    Shall yield them little, tell the constable.
MONTJOY. I shall, King Harry. And so fare thee well:
    Thou never shalt hear herald any more. [*Exit.*]

---

[247] Alluding to the plates of brass formerly let into tombstones.

[248] "*Relapse* of mortality" is simply the *falling-back* or *returning* of the mortal body to its original dust.—This high strain must be set down, I think, among the Poet's instances of overboldness. Certainly, nothing but his prodigious momentum of thought and poetry could carry us fairly through such a strain; hardly even that.

KING HENRY V. I fear thou'lt once more come again for ransom.

[*Enter the Duke of* YORK.[249]]

YORK. My lord, most humbly on my knee I beg
    The leading of the vaward.[250]
KING HENRY V. Take it, brave York.—Now, soldiers, march away:—
    And how thou pleasest, God, dispose the day! [*Exeunt.*]

SCENE IV.

The Field of Battle.

[*Alarum*: excursions. *Enter French Soldier*, PISTOL, *and the Boy.*]

PISTOL. Yield, cur!
FRENCH SOLDIER. *Je pense que vous etes gentilhomme de bonne*
    qualité.
PISTOL. Quality! *Callino, castore me!*[251] art thou a gentleman? what is
    thy name? discuss.
FRENCH SOLDIER. *O Seigneur Dieu!*
PISTOL. O, Signieur Dew should be a gentleman:
    Perpend my words, O Signieur Dew, and mark;
    O Signieur Dew, thou diest on point of fox,[252]
    Except, O signieur, thou do give to me
    Egregious ransom.
FRENCH SOLDIER. O, prenez misericorde! ayez pitie de moi!
PISTOL. Moy[253] shall not serve; I will have forty moys;
    Or I will fetch thy rim[254] out at thy throat

---

[249] This *Edward* Duke of York was the son of Edmund of Langley, the Duke of York, who was the fourth son of King Edward III. He is the man who figures as *Aumerle* in *King Richard the Second.*

[250] The *vaward* is the *vanguard.* So in Holinshed: "He appointed a *vaward*, of the which he made capteine Edward duke of York, who of an haultie courage had desired that office."

[251] These words, it seems, were the burden of an old song. Boswell found the notes in Playford's *Musical Companion.* He says the words mean "Little girl of my heart, for ever and ever"; and adds, "They have, it is true, no great connection with the poor Frenchman's supplications, nor were they meant to have any. Pistol, instead of attending to him, contemptuously hums a tune."

[252] *Fox* was an old fancy-term for *sword.* "The name," says Staunton, "was given from the circumstance that Andrea Ferrara, and, since his time, other foreign sword-cutlers, adopted a fox as the blade-mark of their weapons. Swords, with a running fox rudely engraved on the blades, are still occasionally to be met with in the old curiosity-shops of London."

[253] *Moy* or *moyos* was a measure of corn; in French *muy* or *muid*, Latin *modius*, a bushel. It appears that twenty-seven moys were equal to at least two tons.

In drops of crimson blood.

FRENCH SOLDIER. *Est-il impossible d'échapper la force de ton bras?*

PISTOL. Brass, cur!
Thou damned and luxurious mountain goat,
Offer'st me brass?

FRENCH SOLDIER. *O pardonnez-moi!*

PISTOL. Say'st thou me so? is that a ton of moys?—
Come hither, boy: ask me this slave in French
What is his name.

BOY. *Ecoutez: comment êtes-vous appelé?*

FRENCH SOLDIER. *Monsieur le Fer.*

BOY. He says his name is Master Fer.

PISTOL. Master Fer! I'll fer him, and firk[255] him, and ferret him: discuss the same in French unto him.

BOY. I do not know the French for *fer*, and *ferret*, and *firk*.

PISTOL. Bid him prepare; for I will cut his throat.

FRENCH SOLDIER. *Que dit-il, monsieur?*

BOY. *Il me commande de vous dire que vous faites vous prêt; car ce soldat ici est disposé tout à cette heure de couper votre gorge.*

PISTOL. *Oui, couper la gorge, par ma foi,*
Peasant, unless thou give me crowns, brave crowns;
Or mangled shalt thou be by this my sword.

FRENCH SOLDIER. *O, je vous supplie, pour l'amour de Dieu, me pardonner! Je suis gentilhomme de bonne maison: gardez ma vie, et je vous donnerai deux cents écus.*

PISTOL. What are his words?

BOY. He prays you to save his life: he is a gentleman of a good house; and for his ransom he will give you two hundred crowns.

PISTOL. Tell him my fury shall abate, and I the crowns will take.

FRENCH SOLDIER. *Petit monsieur, que dit-il?*

BOY. *Encore qu'il est contre son jurement de pardoner aucun prisonnier, néanmoins, pour les écus que vous l'avez promis, il est content de vous donner la liberté, le franchisement.*

FRENCH SOLDIER. *Sur mes genoux je vous donne mille remercimens; et je m'estime heureux que je suis tombé entre les mains d'un chevalier, je pense, le plus brave, vaillant, et très distingué seigneur d'Angleterre.*

PISTOL. Expound unto me, boy.

BOY. He gives you, upon his knees, a thousand thanks; and he esteems

---

[254] Pistol is not very scrupulous in his language: he uses *rim* for the *intestines* generally. Bishop Wilkins defines it "the membrane of the belly"; Florio makes it the omentum, "a fat pannicle, caule, sewet, *rim*, or kell wherein the bowels are lapt."

[255] To *firk* is to beat or scourge: to *yerk* and to *jerk* have the same import.—To *ferret* is of kindred meaning, the ferret being a very fierce and spiteful animal. So in the old play of *King Leir*: "I'll *ferret* you ere night for that word."

himself happy that he hath fallen into the hands of one, as he thinks, the most brave, valorous, and thrice-worthy signieur of England.

PISTOL. As I suck blood, I will some mercy show.—

Follow me, cur. [*Exit.*]

BOY. Suivez-vous le grand capitaine. [*Exit French Soldier.*]—I did never know so full a voice issue from so empty a heart: but the saying is true *The empty vessel makes the greatest sound.* Bardolph and Nym had ten times more valour than this roaring devil i' the old play,[256] that every one may pare his nails with a wooden dagger; and they are both hanged; and so would this be, if he durst steal any thing adventurously. I must stay with the lackeys, with the luggage of our camp: the French might have a good prey of us, if he knew of it; for there is none to guard it but boys. [*Exit.*]

SCENE V.

Another Part of the Field of Battle.

[*Enter the Constable,* ORLEANS, BOURBON, *the* Dauphin, *and* RAMBURES, *and others.*]

CONSTABLE. *O diable!*

ORLEANS. *O seigneur! le jour est perdu, tout est perdu!*

DAUPHIN. *Mort de ma vie!*[257] all is confounded, all!

Reproach and everlasting shame

Sits mocking in our plumes. *O mérchante fortune!*—

Do not run away. [*A short alarum.*]

CONSTABLE. Why, all our ranks are broke.

DAUPHIN. O perdurable shame!—let's stab ourselves.

Be these the wretches that we play'd at dice for?

ORLEANS. Is this the King we sent to for his ransom?

BOURBON. Shame and eternal shame, nothing but shame!

Let us die in honour: once more back again;

And he that will not follow Bourbon now,

---

[256] The Devil was a prominent personage in the old Miracle-plays and Moral-plays. He was as turbulent, boisterous, and vainglorious as Pistol. *Ho, ho!* and *Ah, ha!* were among his stereotyped exclamations or *roarings.* The Vice used to belabour him with various indignities, and, among them, threaten to pare his nails with the dagger of lath; the Devil choosing to keep his claws long and sharp.

[257] Ludicrous as these introductory scraps of French appear, so instantly followed by good, nervous mother-English, yet they are judicious, and produce the impression Shakespeare intended: a sudden feeling struck at once on the ears, as well as the eyes, of the audience, that" here come the French, the baffled French braggards!" And this will appear the more judicious, when we reflect on the scanty apparatus of distinguishing dresses in Shakespeare's tiring-room.—COLERIDGE.

Let him go hence, and with his cap in hand,
Like a base pander, hold the chamber-door
Whilst by a slave, no gentler than my dog,[258]
His fairest daughter is contaminated.
CONSTABLE. Disorder, that hath spoil'd us, friend us now!
Let us on heaps[259] go offer up our lives.
ORLEANS. We are enow yet living in the field
To smother up the English in our throngs,
If any order might be thought upon.
BOURBON. The devil take order now! I'll to the throng:
Let life be short; else shame will be too long. [*Exeunt.*]

SCENE VI.

Another Part of the Field.

[*Alarums. Enter* KING HENRY *and Forces,* EXETER, *and others.*]

KING HENRY V. Well have we done, thrice valiant countrymen:
But all's not done; yet keep the French the field.
EXETER. The Duke of York commends him to your majesty.
KING HENRY V. Lives he, good uncle? thrice within this hour
I saw him down; thrice up again and fighting;
From helmet to the spur all blood he was.
EXETER. In which array, brave soldier, doth he lie,
Larding the plain;[260] and by his bloody side,
Yoke-fellow to his honour-owing wounds,
The noble Earl of Suffolk also lies.
Suffolk first died: and York, all haggled over,
Comes to him, where in gore he lay insteep'd,
And takes him by the beard; kisses the gashes
That bloodily did spawn upon his face;
And cries aloud *Tarry, dear cousin Suffolk!*
My soul shall thine keep company to heaven;
Tarry, sweet soul, for mine, then fly abreast,
As in this glorious and well-foughten field
We kept together in our chivalry!
Upon these words I came and cheer'd him up:
He smiled me in the face, raught[261] me his hand,

---

[258] That is, having no *more gentility*, no *higher rank*, than my dog.

[259] *On heaps* is *in crowds*. Repeatedly so.

[260] That is, *enriching* the plain with his blood. In *1 Henry the Fourth*, ii. 2, Falstaff is said to do the same thing with his sweat: "Fat Falstaff sweats to death, and *lards* the lean earth as he walks along."

And, with a feeble gripe, says, *Dear my lord,*
Commend my service to me sovereign.
So did he turn and over Suffolk's neck
He threw his wounded arm and kiss'd his lips;
And so espoused to death, with blood he seal'd
A testament of noble-ending love.
The pretty and sweet manner of it forced
Those waters from me which I would have stopp'd;
But[262] I had not so much of man in me,
And all my mother came into mine eyes
And gave me up to tears.
KING HENRY V. I blame you not;
For, hearing this, I must perforce compound
With mistful eyes, or they will issue too. [*Alarum.*]
But, hark! what new alarum is this same?—
The French have reinforced their scatter'd men:
Then every soldier kill his prisoners:
Give the word through. [*Exeunt.*]

SCENE VII.

Another Part of the Field.

[*Alarums. Enter* FLUELLEN *and* GOWER.]

FLUELLEN. Kill the poys and the luggage! 'tis expressly against the
law of arms: 'tis as arrant a piece of knavery, mark you now, as
can be offer't; in your conscience, now, is it not?

GOWER. 'Tis certain there's not a boy left alive; and the cowardly
rascals that ran from the battle ha' done this slaughter: besides,
they have burned and carried away all that was in the King's tent;
wherefore the King, most worthily, hath caused every soldier to cut
his prisoner's throat.[263] O, 'tis a gallant King!

FLUELLEN. Ay, he was porn at Monmouth, Captain Gower. What call
you the town's name where Alexander the Pig was born!

GOWER. Alexander the Great.

FLUELLEN. Why, I pray you, is not pig great? the pig, or the great, or

---

[261] *Raught* is the old preterit of *reach.*

[262] *But* here is equivalent to *but that.* A frequent usage.

[263] This incident is related in full by Holinshed. It appears afterwards, however, that
the King, on finding that the danger was not so great as he at first thought, stopped the
slaughter, and was able to save a great number. It is observable that the King gives as his
reason for the order, that he expected another battle, and had not men enough to guard
one army and fight another. Gower here assigns a different reason. Holinshed gives both
reasons, and the Poet chose to put one in the King's mouth, the other in Gower's.

the mighty, or the huge, or the magnanimous, are all one reckonings, save the phrase is a little variations.

GOWER. I think Alexander the Great was born in Macedon; his father was called Philip of Macedon, as I take it.

FLUELLEN. I think it is in Macedon where Alexander is porn. I tell you, captain, if you look in the maps of the 'orld, I warrant you sall find, in the comparisons between Macedon and Monmouth, that the situations, look you, is both alike. There is a river in Macedon; and there is also moreover a river at Monmouth: it is called Wye at Monmouth; but it is out of my prains what is the name of the other river; but 'tis all one, 'tis alike as my fingers is to my fingers, and there is salmons in both. If you mark Alexander's life well, Harry of Monmouth's life is come after it indifferent well;[264] for there is figures in all things. Alexander,—God knows, and you know, in his rages, and his furies, and his wraths, and his cholers, and his moods, and his displeasures, and his indignations, and also being a little intoxicates in his prains, did, in his ales and his angers, look you, kill his best friend, Cleitus.

GOWER. Our King is not like him in that: he never killed any of his friends.

FLUELLEN. It is not well done, mark you now take the tales out of my mouth, ere it is made and finished. I speak but in the figures and comparisons of it: as Alexander killed his friend Cleitus, being in his ales and his cups; so also Harry Monmouth, being in his right wits and his good judgments, turned away the fat knight with the great belly-doublet:[265] he was full of jests, and gipes, and knaveries, and mocks; I have forgot his name.

GOWER. Sir John Falstaff.

FLUELLEN. That is he: I'll tell you there is good men porn at Monmouth.

GOWER. Here comes his majesty.

[*Alarum. Enter* KING HENRY, *with a part of the English Forces;* WARWICK, GLOUCESTER, EXETER, *and others.*]

KING HENRY V. I was not angry since I came to France
 Until this instant.—Take a trumpet, herald;
 Ride thou unto the horsemen on yon hill:
 If they will fight with us, bid them come down,
 Or void the field; they do offend our sight:
 If they'll do neither, we will come to them,

---

[264] "*Indifferent* well" is *tolerably* well.

[265] That is, "*great-bellied* doublet," which was the opposite of "thin-bellied doublet." *Doublet* was the name of a man's upper garment.

And make them skirr away,[266] as swift as stones
Enforced from the old Assyrian slings:
Besides, we'll cut the throats of those we have,
And not a man of them that we shall take
Shall taste our mercy. Go and tell them so.

[*Enter* MONTJOY.]

EXETER. Here comes the herald of the French, my liege.
GLOUCESTER. His eyes are humbler than they used to be.
KING HENRY V. How now! what means this, herald? know'st thou not
    That I have fined these bones of mine for ransom?
    Comest thou again for ransom?
MONTJOY. No, great King:
    I come to thee for charitable licence,
    That we may wander o'er this bloody field
    To look our dead,[267] and then to bury them;
    To sort our nobles from our common men.
    For many of our princes—woe the while!—
    Lie drown'd and soak'd in mercenary blood;
    So do our vulgar drench their peasant limbs
    In blood of princes; and their wounded steeds
    Fret fetlock deep in gore and with wild rage
    Jerk out their armed heels at their dead masters,
    Killing them twice. O, give us leave, great King,
    To view the field in safety and dispose
    Of their dead bodies!
KING HENRY V. I tell thee truly, herald,
    I know not if the day be ours or no;
    For yet a many of your horsemen peer
    And gallop o'er the field.
MONTJOY. The day is yours.
KING HENRY V. Praised be God, and not our strength, for it!
    What is this castle call'd that stands hard by?
MONTJOY. They call it Agincourt.
KING HENRY V. Then call we this the field of Agincourt,
    Fought on the day of Crispin Crispianus.
FLUELLEN. Your grandfather of famous memory, an't please your
    majesty, and your great-uncle Edward the Plack Prince of Wales,
    as I have read in the chronicles, fought a most prave pattle here in

---

    [266] *Scour* away; to run swiftly in various directions. It has the same meaning in
Macbeth, v. 3, "*Skirr* the country round."
    [267] The use of *look* as a transitive verb was not uncommon. The incident is thus
related by Holinshed: "In the morning Montjoie and foure other heralds came to the king,
to know the number of prisoners, and to desire buriall for the dead."

France.

KING HENRY V. They did, Fluellen.

FLUELLEN. Your majesty says very true: if your majesties is remembered of it, the Welshmen did good service in a garden where leeks did grow, wearing leeks in their Monmouth caps;[268] which, your majesty know, to this hour is an honourable badge of the service; and I do believe your majesty takes no scorn to wear the leek upon Saint Tavy's day.

KING HENRY V. I wear it for a memorable honour;
For I am Welsh, you know, good countryman.

FLUELLEN. All the water in Wye cannot wash your majesty's Welsh plood out of your pody, I can tell you that: God pless it and preserve it, as long as it pleases his grace, and his majesty too!

KING HENRY V. Thanks, good my countryman.

FLUELLEN. By Jeshu, I am your majesty's countryman, I care not who know it; I will confess it to all the 'orld: I need not to be ashamed of your majesty, praised be God, so long as your majesty is an honest man.

KING HENRY V. God keep me so!—Our heralds go with him:
Bring me just notice of the numbers dead
On both our parts.—Call yonder fellow hither.

[*Points to* WILLIAMS. *Exeunt Heralds with* MONTJOY.]

EXETER. Soldier, you must come to the King.

KING HENRY V. Soldier, why wearest thou that glove in thy cap?

WILLIAMS. An't please your majesty, 'tis the gage of one that I should fight withal, if he be alive.

KING HENRY V. An Englishman?

WILLIAMS. An't please your majesty, a rascal that swaggered with me last night; who, if alive and ever dare to challenge this glove, I have sworn to take him a box o' th' ear: or if I can see my glove in his cap, which he swore, as he was a soldier, he would wear if alive, I will strike it out soundly.

KING HENRY V. What think you, Captain Fluellen? is it fit this soldier keep his oath?

FLUELLEN. He is a craven and a villain else, an't please your majesty, in my conscience.

KING HENRY V. It may be his enemy is a gentleman of great sort,[269]

---

[268] Fuller, in his *Worthies of Monmouthshire*, says, "The best caps were formerly made at Monmouth, where the *cappers'* chapel doth still remain." He adds, "If at this day the phrase *of wearing a Monmouth cap* be taken in a bad acception, I hope the inhabitants of that town will endeavour to disprove the occasion."

[269] *Great sort* is *high rank*. A man of such rank is not bound to *answer* to the challenge from one of the soldier's *low degree*.

quite from the answer of his degree.

FLUELLEN. Though he be as good a gentleman as the devil is, as Lucifer and Beelzebub himself, it is necessary, look your grace, that he keep his vow and his oath: if he be perjured, see you now, his reputation is as arrant a villain and a Jack-sauce,[270] as ever his black shoe trod upon God's ground and his earth, in my conscience, la!

KING HENRY V. Then keep thy vow, sirrah, when thou meetest the fellow.

WILLIAMS. So I will, my liege, as I live.

KING HENRY V. Who servest thou under?

WILLIAMS. Under Captain Gower, my liege.

FLUELLEN. Gower is a good captain, and is good knowledge and literatured in the wars.

KING HENRY V. Call him hither to me, soldier.

WILLIAMS. I will, my liege. [*Exit.*]

KING HENRY V. Here, Fluellen; wear thou this favour for me and stick it in thy cap: when Alençon and myself were down together,[271] I plucked this glove from his helm: if any man challenge this, he is a friend to Alençon, and an enemy to our person; if thou encounter any such, apprehend him, an thou dost me love.

FLUELLEN. Your grace does me as great honours as can be desired in the hearts of his subjects: I would fain see the man, that has but two legs, that shall find himself aggrieved at this glove; that is all; but I would fain see it once, an please God of his grace that I might see.

KING HENRY V. Knowest thou Gower?

FLUELLEN. He is my dear friend, an please you.

KING HENRY V. Pray thee, go seek him, and bring him to my tent.

FLUELLEN. I will fetch him. [*Exit.*]

KING HENRY V. My Lord of Warwick, and my brother Gloucester,
    Follow Fluellen closely at the heels:
    The glove which I have given him for a favour
    May haply purchase him a box o' th' ear;
    It is the soldier's; I by bargain should
    Wear it myself. Follow, good cousin Warwick:
    If that the soldier strike him,—as I judge
    By his blunt bearing he will keep his word,—
    Some sudden mischief may arise of it;
    For I do know Fluellen valiant

---

[270] *Jack-sauce* for *saucy Jack. Jack* was used as a term of contempt.

[271] Henry was felled to the ground by the Duke of Alençon, but recovered, and slew two of the duke's attendants. Alençon was afterwards killed by the King's guard, contrary to Henry's intention, who wished to save him.

And, touched with choler, hot as gunpowder,
And quickly will return an injury:
Follow and see there be no harm between them.—
Go you with me, uncle of Exeter. [*Exeunt.*]

SCENE VIII.

Before KING HENRY'*s Pavilion.*

[*Enter* GOWER *and* WILLIAMS.]

WILLIAMS. I warrant it is to knight you, captain.

[*Enter* FLUELLEN.]

FLUELLEN. God's will and his pleasure, captain, I beseech you now,
    come apace to the King: there is more good toward you
    peradventure than is in your knowledge to dream of.
WILLIAMS. Sir, know you this glove?
FLUELLEN. Know the glove! I know the glove is glove.
WILLIAMS. I know this; and thus I challenge it. [*Strikes him.*]
FLUELLEN. 'Sblood! an arrant traitor as any is in the universal world,
    or in France, or in England!
GOWER. How now, sir! you villain!
WILLIAMS. Do you think I'll be forsworn?
FLUELLEN. Stand away, Captain Gower; I will give treason his
    payment into[272] ploughs, I warrant you.
WILLIAMS. I am no traitor.
FLUELLEN. That's a lie in thy throat.—I charge you in his majesty's
    name, apprehend him: he's a friend of the Duke Alençon's.

[*Enter* WARWICK *and* GLOUCESTER.]

WARWICK. How now, how now! what's the matter?
FLUELLEN. My Lord of Warwick, here is—praised be God for it!—a
    most contagious treason come to light, look you, as you shall
    desire in a summer's day. Here is his majesty.

[*Enter* KING HENRY *and* EXETER.]

KING HENRY V. How now! what's the matter?
FLUELLEN. My liege, here is a villain and a traitor, that, look your
    grace, has struck the glove which your majesty is take out of the

---

[272] *Into* and *in* were often used indiscriminately.

helmet of Alençon.

WILLIAMS. My liege, this was my glove; here is the fellow of it; and he that I gave it to in change promised to wear it in his cap: I promised to strike him, if he did: I met this man with my glove in his cap, and I have been as good as my word.

FLUELLEN. Your majesty hear now, saving your majesty's manhood, what an arrant, rascally, beggarly, lousy knave it is: I hope your majesty is pear me testimony and witness, and will avouchment, that this is the glove of Alençon, that your majesty is give me; in your conscience, now?

KING HENRY V. Give me thy glove,[273] soldier: look, here is the fellow of it.
    'Twas I, indeed, thou promised'st to strike;
    And thou hast given me most bitter terms.

FLUELLEN. An please your majesty, let his neck answer for it, if there is any martial law in the world.

KING HENRY V. How canst thou make me satisfaction?

WILLIAMS. All offences, my lord, come from the heart: never came any from mine that might offend your majesty.

KING HENRY V. It was ourself thou didst abuse.

WILLIAMS. Your majesty came not like yourself: you appeared to me but as a common man; witness the night, your garments, your lowliness; and what your highness suffered under that shape, I beseech you take it for your own fault and not mine: for had you been as I took you for, I made no offence; therefore, I beseech your highness, pardon me.

KING HENRY V. Here, uncle Exeter, fill this glove with crowns,
    And give it to this fellow.—Keep it, fellow;
    And wear it for an honour in thy cap
    Till I do challenge it.—Give him the crowns:—
    And, captain, you must needs be friends with him.

FLUELLEN. By this day and this light, the fellow has mettle enough in his belly.—Hold, there is twelve pence for you; and I pray you to serve Got, and keep you out of prawls, and prabbles' and quarrels, and dissensions, and, I warrant you, it is the better for you.

WILLIAMS. I will none of your money.

FLUELLEN. It is with a good will; I can tell you, it will serve you to mend your shoes: come, wherefore should you be so pashful? your shoes is not so good: 'tis a good shilling, I warrant you, or I will change it.

[*Enter an English Herald.*]

---

[273] Here "*thy* glove" evidently means the glove that Williams has in his cap. The King and Williams had exchanged gloves, so that now each has the other's glove in pledge. But the King has just given to Fluellen the glove he received from Williams; and he now takes from his pocket the mate to the one that Williams received from him.

KING HENRY V. Now, herald, are the dead number'd?
HERALD. Here is the number of the slaughter'd French. [*Delivers a paper.*]
KING HENRY V. What prisoners of good sort are taken, uncle?
EXETER. Charles Duke of Orleans, nephew to the King;
 John Duke of Bourbon, and Lord Bouciqualt:
 Of other lords and barons, knights and squires,
 Full fifteen hundred, besides common men.
KING HENRY V. This note doth tell me of ten thousand French
 That in the field lie slain: of princes, in this number,
 And nobles bearing banners, there lie dead
 One hundred twenty six: added to these,
 Of knights, esquires, and gallant gentlemen,
 Eight thousand and four hundred; of the which,
 Five hundred were but yesterday dubb'd knights:
 So that, in these ten thousand they have lost,
 There are but sixteen hundred mercenaries;[274]
 The rest are princes, barons, lords, knights, squires,
 And gentlemen of blood and quality.
 The names of those their nobles that lie dead:
 Charles Delabreth, High-Constable of France;
 Jaques of Chatillon, admiral of France;
 The master of the cross-bows, Lord Rambures;
 Great Master of France, the brave Sir Guichard Dolphin,
 John Duke of Alençon, Anthony Duke of Brabant,
 The brother of the Duke of Burgundy,
 And Edward Duke of Bar: of lusty earls,
 Grandpre and Roussi, Fauconberg and Foix,
 Beaumont and Marle, Vaudemont and Lestrale.
 Here was a royal fellowship of death!—
 Where is the number of our English dead?—

[*Herald presents another paper.*]

 Edward the Duke of York, the Earl of Suffolk,
 Sir Richard Ketly, Davy Gam,[275] esquire:
 None else of name; and of all other men
 But five and twenty.—O God, thy arm was here;
 And not to us, but to thy arm alone,

---

[274] Mercenaries were soldiers who received pay, as distinguished from such as followed their lords under the obligations of feudal service.

[275] A pleasing anecdote is told of this brave Welshman. Having been sent out before the battle to reconnoitre the enemy, he reported, "May it please you, my liege, there are enough to be killed, enough to be taken prisoners, and enough to run away." It is said that among his other feats at Agincourt he saved the King's life.

Ascribe we all!—When, without stratagem,
But in plain shock and even play of battle,
Was ever known so great and little loss
On one part and on the other?—Take it, God,
For it is none but thine!
EXETER. 'Tis wonderful!
KING HENRY V. Come, go we in procession to the village.
And be it death proclaimed through our host
To boast of this or take the praise from God
Which is his only.
FLUELLEN. Is it not lawful, an please your majesty, to tell how many
is killed?
KING HENRY V. Yes, captain; but with this acknowledgement,
That God fought for us.
FLUELLEN. Yes, my conscience, he did us great good.
KING HENRY V. Do we all holy rites:[276]
Let there be sung *Non nobis* and *Te Deum*;
The dead with charity enclosed in clay:
And then to Calais; and to England then:
Where ne'er from France arrived more happy men. [*Exeunt.*]

SCENE IX.

France. An English Court of Guard.

[*Enter* FLUELLEN *and* GOWER.]

GOWER. Nay, that's right; but why wear you your leek today?
Saint Davy's day is past.
FLUELLEN. There is occasions and causes why and wherefore in all
things: I will tell you, asse my friend, Captain Gower: the rascally,
scald,[277] beggarly, lousy, pragging knave, Pistol,—which you and
yourself and all the world know to be no petter than a fellow, look
you now, of no merits,—he is come to me and prings me pread and
salt yesterday, look you, and bid me eat my leek: it was in place
where I could not breed no contention with him; but I will be so
bold as to wear it in my cap till I see him once again, and then I

---

[276] The king, gathering his army togither, gave thanks to Almightie God for so
happie a victorie, causing his preiats and chapleins to sing this psalme, *In exitu Israel de
Egypto*; and commaunded every man to kneele downe on the ground at this verse, *Non
nobis, Domine, non nobis, sed nomini tuo da gloriam.* Which doone, he caused TE DEUM
with certeine anthems to be soong, giving laud and praise to God, without boasting of his
owne force or anie humane power.—HOLINSHED.

[277] *Scald* is *scurvy* or *scabby*, in its proper meaning; but came to be used as a word
of contempt, implying poverty, disease, and filth.

will tell him a little piece of my desires.

GOWER. Why, here he comes, swelling like a turkey-cock.

FLUELLEN. 'Tis no matter for his swellings nor his turkey-cocks.—

[*Enter* PISTOL.]

Got pless you, Aunchient Pistol! you scurvy, lousy knave, Got pless
    you!

PISTOL. Ha! art thou bedlam? dost thou thirst, base Trojan, To have
    me fold up Parca's fatal web? Hence! I am qualmish at the smell of
    leek.

FLUELLEN. I peseech you heartily, scurvy, lousy knave, at my
    desires, and my requests, and my petitions, to eat, look you, this
    leek: because, look you, you do not love it, nor your affections and
    your appetites and your digestions does not agree with it, I would
    desire you to eat it.

PISTOL. Not for Cadwallader and all his goats.

FLUELLEN. There is one goat for you. [*Strikes him.*] Will you be so
    good, scald knave, as eat it?

PISTOL. Base Trojan, thou shalt die.

FLUELLEN. You say very true, scald knave, when God's will is: I will
    desire you to live in the mean time, and eat your victuals: come,
    there is sauce for it. [*Strikes him again.*] You called me yesterday
    mountain-squire; but I will make you to-day a squire of low
    degree. I pray you, fall to: if you can mock a leek, you can eat a
    leek.

GOWER. Enough, captain: you have astonish'd[278] him.

FLUELLEN. I say, I will make him eat some part of my leek, or I will
    peat his pate four days.—Pite, I pray you; it is good for your green
    wound and your ploody coxcomb.

PISTOL. Must I bite?

FLUELLEN. Yes, certainly, and out of doubt and out of question too,
    and ambiguities.

PISTOL. By this leek, I will most horribly revenge: I eat and eat, I
    swear—

FLUELLEN. Eat, I pray you: will you have some more sauce to your
    leek? there is not enough leek to swear by.

PISTOL. Quiet thy cudgel; thou dost see I eat.

FLUELLEN. Much good do you, scald knave, heartily. Nay, pray you,
    throw none away; the skin is good for your broken coxcomb.
    When you take occasions to see leeks hereafter, I pray you, mock
    at 'em; that is all.

---

[278] That is, *stunned* him, knocked him into confusion and numbness. Such is the
proper meaning of to *astonish*.

PISTOL. Good.

FLUELLEN. Ay, leeks is good: hold you, there is a groat to heal your pate.

PISTOL. Me a groat!

FLUELLEN. Yes, verily and in truth, you shall take it; or I have another leek in my pocket, which you shall eat.

PISTOL. I take thy groat in earnest of revenge.

FLUELLEN. If I owe you any thing, I will pay you in cudgels: you shall be a woodmonger, and buy nothing of me but cudgels. God b' wi' you, and keep you, and heal your pate. [*Exit.*]

PISTOL. All hell shall stir for this.

GOWER. Go, go; you are a counterfeit cowardly knave. Will you mock at an ancient tradition, begun upon an honourable respect, and worn as a memorable trophy of predeceased valour and dare not avouch in your deeds any of your words? I have seen you gleeking and galling[279] at this gentleman twice or thrice. You thought, because he could not speak English in the native garb, he could not therefore handle an English cudgel: you find it otherwise; and henceforth let a Welsh correction teach you a good English condition.[280] Fare ye well. [*Exit.*]

PISTOL. Doth Fortune play the huswife[281] with me now?
    News have I, that my Nell is dead i' the spital
    Of malady of France;
    And there my rendezvous is quite cut off.
    Old I do wax; and from my weary limbs
    Honour is cudgelled. Well, bawd I'll turn,
    And something lean to cutpurse of quick hand.
    To England will I steal, and there I'll steal:
    And patches will I get unto these cudgell'd scars,
    And swear I got them in the Gallia wars. [*Exit.*]

ACT V.

[*Enter* CHORUS.]

CHORUS. Vouchsafe to those that have not read the story,
    That I may prompt them: and of such as have,
    I humbly pray them to admit the excuse
    Of time, of numbers and due course of things,
    Which cannot in their huge and proper life
    Be here presented. Now we bear the King

---

[279] *Gleeking* is scoffing, *flouting*; and *galling* is here used in a kindred sense,—*venting sarcasms*, things that *irritate*.

[280] *Condition*, as usual, for *temper* or *disposition*.

[281] *Huswife* for *jilt*, or *hussy*, as we have it still in common speech.

Toward Calais: grant him there; there seen,
Heave him away upon your winged thoughts
Athwart the sea. Behold, the English beach
Pales-in[282] the flood with men, with wives and boys,
Whose shouts and claps out-voice the deep mouth'd sea,
Which like a mighty whiffler[283] 'fore the King
Seems to prepare his way: so let him land,
And solemnly[284] see him set on to London.
So swift a pace hath thought that even now
You may imagine him upon Blackheath;
Where-that[285] his lords desire him to have borne
His bruised helmet and his bended sword
Before him through the city: he forbids it,
Being free from vainness and self-glorious pride;
Giving full trophy, signal and ostent,[286]
Quite from himself to God. But now behold,
In the quick forge and working-house of thought,
How London doth pour out her citizens!
The mayor and all his brethren in best sort,—
Like to the senators of the antique Rome,
With the plebeians swarming at their heels,—
Go forth and fetch their conquering Caesar in:
As, by a lower but loving likelihood,
Were now the general of our gracious Empress,—
As in good time he may,—from Ireland coming,
Bringing rebellion broachèd[287] on his sword,
How many would the peaceful city quit,
To welcome him! much more, and much more cause,
Did they this Harry. Now in London place him;
As yet the lamentation of the French
Invites the King of England's stay at home;
The emperor's coming[288] in behalf of France,

---

[282] To *pale-in* is to *fence round* or *enclose with palings.*

[283] *Whiffle* is another form of *whistle,* and was used of a *fife* or *pipe.* As fifers or *pipers* commonly marched at the head of troops and processions, so *whiffler* came to be used of any one who went ahead of another to clear the way.

[284] *Solemnly* is *in* state, or *with ordered pomp and ceremony.* The proper construction is, "see him set on solemnly to London."

[285] *Where-that* is plainly equivalent to *whereas.*

[286] *Ostent* is *show* or *display.*

[287] *Broached is pierced through, transfixed.*—The allusion is to the Earl of Essex, who in April, 1599, set out for Ireland, as Governor, to put down the rebellion of Tyrone. His departure was an occasion of great enthusiasm, people of all ranks thronging around him and showering benedictions upon him. But these bright anticipations were sadly disappointed. The expedition failed utterly; and the Earl's return, in September following, was unhonoured and unmarked.

To order peace between them; and omit
All the occurrences, whatever chanced,
Till Harry's back-return again to France:
There must we bring him; and myself have play'd
The interim, by remembering you 'tis past.
Then brook abridgment, and your eyes advance,
After your thoughts, straight back again to France. [*Exit.*]

SCENE I.

Troyes in Champagne. An Apartment in the French KING'*s Palace.*

[*Enter,   from   one   side,*   KING   HENRY,   BEDFORD,
GLOUCESTER,   EXETER,   WARWICK,   WESTMORE-
LAND, *and other Lords*; *from the other side, the French*
KING, QUEEN ISABEL, *the* PRINCESS KATHARINE,
ALICE *and   other   Ladies,   and   Lords*; *the   Duke   of*
BURGUNDY, *and his train.*]

KING HENRY V. Peace to this meeting, wherefore we are met![289]—
    Unto our brother France, and to our sister,
    Health and fair time of day;—joy and good wishes
    To our most fair and princely cousin Katharine;—
    And, as a branch and member of this royalty,
    By whom this great assembly is contrived,
    We do salute you, Duke of Burgundy;—
    And, princes French, and peers, health to you all!
KING OF FRANCE. Right joyous are we to behold your face,
    Most worthy brother England; fairly met:
    So are you, princes English, every one.
QUEEN ISABEL. So happy be the issue, brother England,
    Of this good day and of this gracious meeting,
    As we are now glad to behold your eyes;
    Your eyes, which hitherto have borne in them
    Against the French, that met them in their bent,
    The fatal balls of murdering basilisks:[290]
    The venom of such looks, we fairly hope,

---

[288] The Emperor Sigismund, who was married to Henry's second cousin, and who visited England at this time.

[289] They have met together for the purpose of knitting up a peace, and the King begins by wishing peace to the meeting. "Peace, for which we are met, be to the meeting."

[290] The *basilisk* was a *serpent* which, it was anciently supposed, could destroy the object of his vengeance by merely looking at it. It was also a *great gun*; and the allusion here is double.

Have lost[291] their quality, and that this day
Shall change all griefs and quarrels into love.
KING HENRY V. To cry amen to that, thus we appear.
QUEEN ISABEL. You English princes all, I do salute you.
BURGUNDY. My duty to you both, on equal love,
Great kings of France and England! That I have labour'd,
With all my wits, my pains and strong endeavours,
To bring your most imperial majesties
Unto this bar[292] and royal interview,
Your mightiness on both parts best can witness.
Since then my office hath so far prevail'd
That, face to face and royal eye to eye,
You have congreeted, let it not disgrace me,
If I demand, before this royal view,
What rub or what impediment there is,
Why that the naked, poor and mangled Peace,
Dear nurse of arts and joyful births,
Should not in this best garden of the world
Our fertile France, put up her lovely visage?
Alas, she hath from France too long been chased,
And all her husbandry doth lie on heaps,
Corrupting in its own fertility.
Her vine, the merry cheerer of the heart,
Unpruned dies; her hedges even-pleach'd,[293]
Like prisoners wildly overgrown with hair,
Put forth disorder'd twigs; her fallow leas
The darnel, hemlock and rank fumitory
Doth root upon, while that the coulter rusts
That should deracinate[294] such savagery;
The even mead, that erst brought sweetly forth
The freckled cowslip, burnet and green clover,
Wanting the scythe, all uncorrected, rank,
Conceives by idleness and nothing teems
But hateful docks, rough thistles, kecksies, burs,
Losing both beauty and utility.

---

[291] Here the verb is made to agree with the nearest substantive, *looks*, instead of with its proper nominative, *venom*. Shakespeare has many like instances of false concord. See page 11, note 225.

[292] That is, this *place of congress*. *Bar* is a shortened form of *barrier*. Ordinarily, when sovereigns were to meet in the field for such purposes, a barrier was erected at the place agreed upon, as a protection of either party against the possible violence or treachery of the other. Hence *bar* came to be used for any place of meeting.

[293] *Pleached, plaited, platted* are all words of the same meaning, like the Latin *plicitum*; *folded together*, or *interwoven*. So in *Much Ado About Nothing*, iii. 1; "The *pleached* bower, where honeysuckles, ripened by the sun, forbid the sun to enter."

[294] To *deracinate* is to force up by the roots.

And as our vineyards, fallows, meads and hedges,
Defective in their natures,[295] grow to wildness,
Even so our houses and ourselves and children
Have lost, or do not learn for want of time,
The sciences that should become our country;
But grow like savages,—as soldiers will
That nothing do but meditate on blood,—
To swearing and stern looks, defused[296] attire
And every thing that seems unnatural.
Which to reduce into our former favour,[297]
You are assembled: and my speech entreats
That I may know the let,[298] why gentle Peace
Should not expel these inconveniences
And bless us with her former qualities.

KING HENRY V. If, Duke of Burgundy, you would the peace,
Whose want gives growth to the imperfections
Which you have cited, you must buy that peace
With full accord to all our just demands;
Whose tenors and particular effects
You have enscheduled briefly in your hands.

BURGUNDY. The King hath heard them; to the which as yet
There is no answer made.

KING HENRY V. Well then the peace,
Which you before so urged, lies in his answer.

KING OF FRANCE. I have but with a cursorary[299] eye
O'erglanced the articles: pleaseth your grace
To appoint some of your council presently
To sit with us once more, with better heed
To re-survey them, we will suddenly
Pass our accept[300] and peremptory answer.

KING HENRY V. Brother, we shall.—Go, uncle Exeter,—
And brother Clarence,—and you, brother Gloucester,—
Warwick,—and Huntingdon,[301]—go with the King;

---

[295] Not defective in their *productive* virtue, for they grew to wildness; but defective in their *proper* virtue, which was to serve man with food and support.

[296] It appears from Florio's *Dictionary*, that *defused*, or *diffused*, was used for *confused, defused attire* is therefore *disordered* or *dishevelled attire.*

[297] *Favour* here means comeliness of appearance.—To *reduce* is to *restore* or *bring back*; a sense of the word now obsolete, but legitimate from the Latin *reduco.*

[298] This is the ancient *let*, meaning *hindrance* or *obstruction.*

[299] *Cursorary* appears to be a word of the Poet's own coining, no other instance of it being known. *Cursory* had not syllables enough for the place.

[300] *Suddenly* in the sense of *quickly* or *speedily*. Often so. To *pass*, as the word is here used, is, apparently, to *fix, conclude*, or *agree upon*. So in *The Taming of the* Shrew, iv. 2: "To *pass* assurance of a dower in marriage." *Accept*, if the text be right, is merely a shortened form of *acceptance.* Shakespeare uses the same freedom in many words.

And take with you free power to ratify,
Augment, or alter, as your wisdoms best
Shall see advantageable[302] for our dignity,
Any thing in or out of our demands,
And we'll consign thereto.—Will you, fair sister,
Go with the princes, or stay here with us?
QUEEN ISABEL. Our gracious brother, I will go with them:
Haply a woman's voice may do some good,
When articles too nicely urged be stood on.
KING HENRY V. Yet leave our cousin Katharine here with us:
She is our capital demand, comprised
Within the fore-rank of our articles.
QUEEN ISABEL. She hath good leave.

[*Exeunt all but* HENRY, KATHARINE, *and* ALICE.]

KING HENRY V. Fair Katharine, and most fair,
Will you vouchsafe to teach a soldier terms
Such as will enter at a lady's ear
And plead his love-suit to her gentle heart?
KATHARINE.
Your majesty shall mock at me; I cannot speak your England.
KING HENRY V. O fair Katharine, if you will love me soundly with
your French heart, I will be glad to hear you confess it brokenly
with your English tongue. Do you like me, Kate?
KATHARINE. *Pardonnez-moi*, I cannot tell vat is *like me.*
KING HENRY V. An angel is like you, Kate, and you are like an
angel.
KATHARINE. *Que dit-il? que je suis semblable à les anges?*
ALICE. *Oui, vraiment, sauf votre grace, ainsi dit-il.*
KING HENRY V. I said so, dear Katharine; and I must not blush to
affirm it.
KATHARINE. *O bon Dieu! les langues des hommes sont pleines de
tromperies.*
KING HENRY V. What says she, fair one? that the tongues of men are
full of deceits?
ALICE. *Oui*, dat de tongues of de mans is be full of deceits,—dat is de
princess.
KING HENRY V. The princess is the better Englishwoman.—I'faith,

---

[301] John Holland, Earl of Huntington, who afterwards married the widow of
Edmund Mortimer, Earl of March. Neither Huntingdon nor Clarence is in the list of
Dramatis Personæ, as neither of them speaks a word.

[302] *Advantageable* for *advantageous*, just as, elsewhere, *disputable* for *disputatious.*
This confusion of active and passive forms, both in adjectives and participles, occurs very
often.

Kate, my wooing is fit for thy understanding: I am glad thou canst
speak no better English; for, if thou couldst, thou wouldst find me
such a plain King that thou wouldst think I had sold my farm to
buy my crown. I know no ways to mince it in love, but directly to
say *I love you*: then if you urge me farther than to say *Do you in
faith*? I wear out my suit. Give me your answer; i'faith, do: and so
clap hands and a bargain: how say you, lady?

KATHARINE. *Sauf votre Honneur*, me understand well.

KING HENRY V. Marry, if you would put me to verses or to dance for
your sake, Kate, why you undid me: for the one, I have neither
words nor measure, and for the other, I have no strength in
measure,³⁰³ yet a reasonable measure in strength. If I could win a
lady at leap-frog, or by vaulting into my saddle with my armour on
my back, under the correction of bragging be it spoken. I should
quickly leap into a wife. Or if I might buffet for my love, or bound
my horse for her favours, I could lay on like a butcher and sit like a
jack-an-apes, never off. But, before God, Kate, I cannot look
greenly nor gasp out my eloquence, nor I have no cunning in
protestation; only downright oaths, which I never use till urged,
nor never break for urging. If thou canst love a fellow of this
temper, Kate,—whose face is not worth sun-burning, that never
looks in his glass for love of any thing he sees there,—let thine eye
be thy cook. I speak to thee plain soldier: If thou canst love me for
this, take me: if not, to say to thee that I shall die, is true; but for
thy love, by the Lord, no; yet I love thee too. And while thou
livest, dear Kate, take a fellow of plain and uncoined constancy;³⁰⁴
for he perforce must do thee right, because he hath not the gift to
woo in other places: for these fellows of infinite tongue, that can
rhyme themselves into ladies' favours, they do always reason
themselves out again. What! a speaker is but a prater; a rhyme is
but a ballad. A good leg will fall;³⁰⁵ a straight back will stoop; a
black beard will turn white; a curled pate will grow bald; a fair
face will wither; a full eye will wax hollow: but a good heart, Kate,
is the sun and the moon; or, rather, the sun, and not the moon; for it
shines bright and never changes, but keeps his course truly. If thou
would have such a one, take me; and take me, take a soldier; take a
soldier, take a King. And what sayest thou then to my love? speak,
my fair, and fairly, I pray thee.

KATHARINE. Is it possible dat I sould love de enemy of France?

---

³⁰³ *Measure* is here used in the sense of *dancing*. To *tread* or *dance* a measure, was
a common phrase.

³⁰⁴ *Uncoined constancy* probably means an affection that has never "gone forth"; a
heart like virgin gold, that has never had any image stamped upon it.

³⁰⁵ Will *fall away*, leaving "his youthful hose a world too wide for his shrunk
shank."

KING HENRY V. No; it is not possible you should love the enemy of France, Kate: but, in loving me, you should love the friend of France; for I love France so well that I will not part with a village of it; I will have it all mine: and, Kate, when France is mine and I am yours, then yours is France and you are mine.

KATHARINE. I cannot tell vat is dat.

KING HENRY V. No, Kate? I will tell thee in French; which I am sure will hang upon my tongue like a new-married wife about her husband's neck, hardly to be shook off. *Quand sur le possession de France, et quand vous avez le possession de moi,*—let me see, what then? Saint Denis be my speed!—*donc votre est France et vous êtes mienne.* It is as easy for me, Kate, to conquer the kingdom as to speak so much more French: I shall never move thee in French, unless it be to laugh at me.

KATHARINE. *Sauf votre Honneur, le Français que vous parlez, il est meilleur que l'Anglais lequel je parle.*

KING HENRY V. No, faith, is't not, Kate: but thy speaking of my tongue, and I thine, most truly-falsely, must needs be granted to be much at one. But, Kate, dost thou understand thus much English, canst thou love me?

KATHARINE. I cannot tell.

KING HENRY V. Can any of your neighbours tell, Kate? I'll ask them. Come, I know thou lovest me: and at night, when you come into your closet, you'll question this gentlewoman about me; and I know, Kate, you will to her dispraise those parts in me that you love with your heart: but, good Kate, mock me mercifully; the rather, gentle princess, because I love thee cruelly. If ever thou beest mine, Kate,—as I have a saving faith within me tells me thou shalt,—I get thee with scrambling, and thou must therefore needs prove a good soldier-breeder: shall not thou and I, between Saint Denis and Saint George, compound a boy, half French, half English, that shall go to Constantinople and take the Turk by the beard? shall we not? what sayest thou, my fair flower-de-luce?

KATHARINE. I do not know dat

KING HENRY V. No; 'tis hereafter to know, but now to promise: do but now promise, Kate, you will endeavour for your French part of such a boy; and for my English moiety take the word of a King and a bachelor. How answer you, *la plus belle Katharine du monde, mon très-cherè et divine déesse?*

KATHARINE. Your *Majesté* ave *fausse* French enough to deceive de most *sage demoiselle* dat is *en France.*

KING HENRY V. Now, fie upon my false French! By mine honour, in true English, I love thee, Kate: by which honour I dare not swear thou lovest me; yet my blood begins to flatter me that thou dost, notwithstanding the poor and untempering effect of my visage.

Now, beshrew my father's ambition! he was thinking of civil wars when he got me: therefore was I created with a stubborn outside, with an aspect of iron, that, when I come to woo ladies, I fright them. But, in faith, Kate, the elder I wax, the better I shall appear: my comfort is, that old age, that ill layer up of beauty, can do no more, spoil upon my face: thou hast me, if thou hast me, at the worst; and thou shalt wear me, if thou wear me, better and better: and therefore tell me, most fair Katharine, will you have me? Put off your maiden blushes; avouch the thoughts of your heart with the looks of an empress; take me by the hand, and say *Harry of England I am thine*: which word thou shalt no sooner bless mine ear withal, but I will tell thee aloud *England is thine, Ireland is thine, France is thine, and Harry Plantagenet is thine*; who though I speak it before his face, if he be not fellow with the best King, thou shalt find the best King of good fellows. Come, your answer in broken music,[306] for thy voice is music and thy English broken; therefore, queen of all, Katharine, break thy mind to me in broken English; wilt thou have me?

KATHARINE. Dat is as it sall please de *roi mon père.*

KING HENRY V. Nay, it will please him well, Kate,—it shall please him, Kate.

KATHARINE. Den it sall also content me.

KING HENRY V. Upon that I kiss your hand, and I call you my queen.

KATHARINE. *Laissez, mon seigneur, laissez, laissez: ma foi, je ne veux point que vous abaissiez votre grandeur en baisant la main d'une de votre seigeurie indigne serviteur; excusez-moi, je vous supplie, mon très-puissant seigneur.*

KING HENRY V. Then I will kiss your lips, Kate.

KATHARINE. *Les dames et demoiselles pour etre baisées devant leur noces, il n'est pas la coutume de France.*

KING HENRY V. Madam my interpreter, what says she?

ALICE. Dat it is not be de fashion *pour les* ladies of France,—I cannot tell vat is *baiser* en Anglish.

KING HENRY V. To kiss.

ALICE. Your majesty *entendre* bettre *que moi.*

KING HENRY V. It is not a fashion for the maids in France to kiss before they are married, would she say?

ALICE. *Oui, vraiment.*

KING HENRY V. O Kate, nice[307] customs curtsy to great kings. Dear Kate, you and I cannot be confined within the weak list[308] of a country's fashion: we are the makers of manners, Kate; and the

---

[306] "*Broken music*" is said to have meant the music of such instruments as lutes, harps, &c.

[307] *Nice* here is *squeamish, scrupulous, fastidious.*

[308] *Weak list* is *slight barrier*; from the language of the tilt-yard.

liberty that follows our places stops the mouth of all find-faults,—
as I will do yours, for upholding the nice fashion of your country in
denying me a kiss: therefore, patiently and yielding. [*Kissing her.*]
You have witchcraft in your lips, Kate: there is more eloquence in
a sugar touch of them than in the tongues of the French council;
and they should sooner persuade Harry of England than a general
petition of monarchs. Here comes your father.

[*Re-enter the French* KING *and his Queen,* BURGUNDY,
BEDFORD, GLOSTER, EXETER, WARWICK,
WESTMORELAND, *&c.*]

BURGUNDY. God save your majesty! my royal cousin, teach you our
princess English?
KING HENRY V. I would have her learn, my fair cousin, how
perfectly I love her; and that is good English.
BURGUNDY. Is she not apt?
KING HENRY V. Our tongue is rough, coz, and my condition is not
smooth; so that, having neither the voice nor the heart of flattery
about me, I cannot so conjure up the spirit of love in her, that he
will appear in his true likeness.
BURGUNDY. Pardon the frankness of my mirth, if I answer you for
that. If you would conjure in her, you must make a circle;[309] if
conjure up love in her in his true likeness, he must appear naked
and blind. Can you blame her then, being a maid yet rosed over
with the virgin crimson of modesty, if she deny the appearance of a
naked blind boy in her naked seeing self? It were, my lord, a hard
condition for a maid to consign to.
KING HENRY V. Yet they do wink and yield, as love is blind and
enforces.
BURGUNDY. They are then excused, my lord, when they see not what
they do.
KING HENRY V. Then, good my lord, teach your cousin to consent
winking.
BURGUNDY. I will wink on her to consent, my lord, if you will teach
her to know my meaning: for maids, well summered and warm
kept, are like flies at Bartholomew-tide,[310] blind, though they have
their eyes; and then they will endure handling, which before would
not abide looking on.

---

[309] Conjurers used to mark out a circle on the ground, within which their conjuring
was to take effect by the appearance of the beings invoked. Probably an equivoque is here
intended, circle being also used for *crown*.
[310] The feast of St. Bartholomew falls on the 24th of August.—Being unskilled in
entomology, I cannot vouch for the scientific accuracy of the text.

KING HENRY V. This moral[311] ties me over to time and a hot summer; and so I shall catch the fly, your cousin, in the latter end and she must be blind too.

BURGUNDY. As love is, my lord, before it loves.

KING HENRY V. It is so: and you may, some of you, thank love for my blindness, who cannot see many a fair French city for one fair French maid that stands in my way.

FRENCH KING. Yes, my lord, you see them perspectively, the cities turned into a maid;[312] for they are all girdled with maiden walls that war hath never entered.

KING HENRY V. Shall Kate be my wife?

FRENCH KING. So please you.

KING HENRY V. I am content; so the maiden cities you talk of may wait on her: so the maid that stood in the way for my wish shall show me the way to my will.

FRENCH KING. We have consented to all terms of reason.

KING HENRY V. Is't so, my lords of England?

WESTMORELAND. The King hath granted every article:
His daughter first, and then in sequel all,
According to their firm proposed natures.

EXETER. Only he hath not yet subscribed this:
Where your majesty demands, that the King of France, having any occasion to write for matter of grant, shall name your highness in this form and with this addition in French, *Notre trescher fils Henri, Roi d'Angleterre, héritier de France*; and thus in Latin, *Præclarissimus*[313] *filius noster Henricus, Rex Angliæ, et hæres Franciæ.*

FRENCH KING. Nor this I have not, brother, so denied,
But your request shall make me let it pass.

KING HENRY V. I pray you then, in love and dear alliance,
Let that one article rank with the rest;
And thereupon give me your daughter.

FRENCH KING. Take her, fair son, and from her blood raise up
Issue to me; that the contending kingdoms
Of France and England, whose very shores look pale
With envy of each other's happiness,

---

[311] A *moral* is the *meaning* or *application* of a fable or apologue.

[312] Perspectives were glasses or instruments to look through, such being the proper meaning of the word. They were of various kinds, and some, it seems, played rather queer pranks with the object looked at. One kind is thus spoken of in *Humane Industry*, 1651: "A picture of the chancellor of France presented to the common beholder a multitude of little faces; but if one did look at it through a *perspective*, there appeared only a single pourtraiture of the chancellor."

[313] *Præclarissimus* for *Præcarissimus*. Shakespeare followed Holinshed, in whose Chronicle it stands thus. Indeed, all the old historians have the same blunder. In the original treaty of Troyes, printed in Rymer, it is *præcarissimus*.

> May cease their hatred, and this dear conjunction
> Plant neighbourhood and Christian-like accord
> In their sweet bosoms, that never war advance
> His bleeding sword 'twixt England and fair France.

ALL. Amen!

KING HENRY V. Now, welcome, Kate;—and bear me witness all,
> That here I kiss her as my sovereign queen. [*Flourish.*]

QUEEN ISABEL. God, the best maker of all marriages,
> Combine your hearts in one, your realms in one!
> As man and wife, being two, are one in love,
> So be there 'twixt your kingdoms such a spousal,
> That never may ill office, or fell jealousy,
> Which troubles oft the bed of blessed marriage,
> Thrust in between the paction[314] of these kingdoms,
> To make divorce of their incorporate league;
> That English may as French, French Englishmen,
> Receive each other.—God speak this Amen!

ALL. Amen!

KING HENRY V. Prepare we for our marriage:—on which day,
> My Lord of Burgundy, we'll take your oath,
> And all the peers', for surety of our league.—
> Then shall I swear to Kate, and you to me;
> And may our oaths well kept and prosperous be!

[*Sennet. Exeunt.*]

[*Enter* CHORUS.]

CHORUS. Thus far, with rough and all-unable pen,
> Our bending[315] author hath pursued the story,
> In little room confining mighty men,
> Mangling by starts the full course of their glory.[316]
> Small time, but in that small most greatly lived
> This star of England: Fortune made his sword;
> By which the world's best garden be achieved,
> And of it left his son imperial lord.
> Henry the Sixth, in infant bands crown'd King
> Of France and England, did this King succeed;
> Whose state so many had the managing,
> That they lost France and made his England bleed:
> Which oft our stage hath shown;[317] and, for their sake,

---

[314] *Paction* is compact, *alliance*, or *league*.

[315] *Bending* beneath the weight of the subject, as being unequal to it.

[316] Giving only *fragments* and *glimpses* of their full career.

In your fair minds let this acceptance take. [*Exit.*]

THE END

---

[317] The three Parts of *King Henry VI.* were written several years before this play, and often acted.

Made in the USA
Middletown, DE
25 January 2018